CAMPAIGN 366

DIEN BIEN PHU 1954

The French Defeat that Lured America into Vietnam

MARTIN WINDROW

ILLUSTRATED BY PETER DENNIS

Series editor Nikolai Bogdanovic

OSPREY PUBLISHING
Bloomsbury Publishing Plc

Kemp House, Chawley Park, Cumnor Hill, Oxford OX2 9PH, UK
29 Earlsfort Terrace, Dublin 2, Ireland
1385 Broadway, 5th Floor, New York, NY 10018, USA
Email: info@ospreypublishing.com
www.ospreypublishing.com

OSPREY is a trademark of Osprey Publishing Ltd

First published in Great Britain in 2021
Transferred to digital print in 2024

A catalogue record for this book is available from the British Library.

Print ISBN: 978 1 4728 4400 2
ePub: 978 1 4728 4401 9
ePDF: 978 1 4728 4398 2
XML: 978 1 4728 4399 9

Maps by www.bounford.com
3D BEVs by Paul Kime
Index by Mark Swift
Typeset by PDQ Digital Media Solutions, Bungay, UK
Printed and bound in India by Replika Press Private Ltd.

24 25 26 27 28   10 9 8 7 6 5 4 3

MIX
Paper from
responsible sources
FSC® C016779
www.fsc.org

Artist's note

Readers may care to note that the original paintings from which the colour
plates in this book were prepared are available for private sale. All
reproduction copyright whatsoever is retained by the publishers. All
enquiries should be addressed to

Peter Dennis, Fieldhead, The Park, Mansfield, Notts, NG18 2AT, UK
Email: magiehollingworth@yahoo.co.uk

The publishers regret that they can enter into no correspondence upon
this matter.

Osprey Publishing supports the Woodland Trust, the UK's leading woodland
conservation charity.

To find out more about our authors and books visit
www.ospreypublishing.com. Here you will find extracts, author
interviews, details of forthcoming events and the option to sign up for
our newsletter.

Dedication

To my late friend Caporal-Chef Georges Gebhardt, 1 BEP – who was lucky
enough to be flown out of Dien Bien Phu as a casualty; and, with great
respect and sincere thanks, to Médecin Col. Dr. Jacques Gindrey, 44 ACM,
who died at the age of 94 on 11 February 2021.

Author's note and acknowledgements

I am grateful for the opportunity to draw upon more recent sources
(particularly the valuable book by Kevin Boylan and Luc Olivier – see
Further Reading) to correct a number of errors in my *The Last Valley*
(Weidenfeld & Nicolson, 2004). The latter is still in print, and naturally
contains a great deal more background history, daily detail, and personal
accounts than is possible in this brief introductory account of the battle.

For reasons of space, the present book also omits peripheral aspects such
as the abortive Operation *Condor* from Laos to extract the Dien Bien Phu
garrison, and the failed diplomatic efforts to secure USAAF intervention.

Every book about Dien Bien Phu inevitably suffers from the fact that no
French photographs left the camp after the airfield was closed on 28 March
1954, but I acknowledge with gratitude the kind assistance of Kieran Lynch,
Simon Dunstan, and Oliver Barnham.

In only one of the maps do we have enough information to attempt to
show any of the developing VPA trench systems. Obviously, these – and
communication trenches dug to link French strongpoints – became
ubiquitous during the April fighting.

Conversion table

Imperial	Metric
1 inch	2.54cm
1 foot	0.3048m
1 yard	0.9144m
1 mile	1.6093km
1 pound	0.4536kg
1 long ton	1.0160t

PREVIOUS PAGE: French troops move around the entrenched
camp under fire. (Keystone/Hulton Archive via Getty Images)

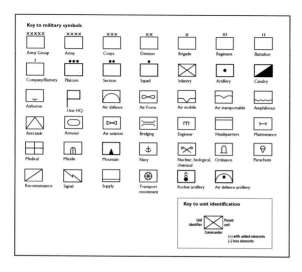

CONTENTS

ORIGINS OF THE CAMPAIGN

STRATEGIC BACKGROUND

When Gen. Henri Navarre arrived in Saigon in May 1953 to take command of the approximately 172,000-strong French Far East Expeditionary Corps (*Corps Expéditionnaire Français d'Extrême-Orient* – CEFEO), the war against the Viet Minh insurgency in Vietnam had been dragging on since November 1946. During those years this largest of France's Indochinese colonies (the others being Laos and Cambodia) had existed under parallel and rival governments. One was French, with local proxies; the other was Ho Chi Minh's Democratic Republic of Vietnam (DRV), which he had proclaimed in Hanoi on 2 September 1945 before the return of French forces imprisoned or driven out by the Japanese.

While guerrilla activity had continued in South and Central Vietnam (Cochinchina and Annam), North Vietnam (Tonkin) had long been the main cockpit of the war between the Vietnam People's Army (VPA) and the CEFEO. Most of it was controlled by the Viet Minh; while the French occasionally mounted mechanized or airborne thrusts into its territory, these could not be sustained for more than a matter of days, and achieved no lasting results. Only the French heartland of the Red River Delta around Hanoi and Haiphong, surrounded by a belt of concrete blockhouses, was secure from conventional (though not from guerrilla) attack, and even there genuine French control did not extend beyond the towns and – by daylight – the main transport routes.

During 1952–53, Gen. Vo Nguyen Giap's VPA main force had multiplied the demands on the CEFEO's reserves by large-scale manoeuvre operations, notably in a thrust westwards through the virtually roadless Thai Highlands around the middle Black River to threaten the weakly defended colony of Laos to the south.[1] This drove out French garrisons, and planted both political infrastructure and stay-behind troops; but the successful French defence of

1   'Thai' in this context refers not to Thailand (Siam), but to several related peoples within the *montagnard* tribal population of north-west Tonkin, who were historically hostile to the Viet Minh.

a largely flown-in garrison with tactical air support at Na San in December 1952 had increased French confidence in the concept of 'air-ground bases'.

Since 1951 the cost of France's war had increasingly been borne by the United States, which had re-equipped the CEFEO and its fledgeling Vietnamese National Army (*Armée Nationale Vietnamienne* – ANV). Although French governments had accepted by 1953 that only a negotiated peace was realistically possible, continued American support depended upon the CEFEO's continued military efforts, particularly in readying the ANV to take over much of the burden (as a step along the road to America's preferred goal of Vietnamese decolonization).

General Navarre's military remit was to win France a favourable bargaining position in eventual peace talks, by inflicting serious defeats on the VPA during 1954–55. Monsoon rains limited both sides' operational possibilities during each April–September, and when anticipating the campaign season of autumn 1953–spring 1954 the intelligence networks of each army strove to deduce their enemy's intentions.

General Navarre wished to maintain a basically defensive stance in Tonkin, committing the bulk of his reserves and much of the ANV to a major amphibious offensive (Operation *Atlante*) down in Annam, where the Viet Minh's integrated politico-military Interzone 5 had virtually cut Vietnam in half. *Atlante* was planned as a series of successive operations intended to last from late January until July 1954; it would progressively involve 53 battalions, nearly half of them ANV.

These assets would dwarf those available in Tonkin. There Gen. Navarre, and his regional deputy Maj.-Gen. René Cogny of Land Forces North Vietnam (*Forces Terrestres Nord-Vietnam* – FTNV), had to defend both the Delta, and the Laos frontier country south of the Black River, against VPA infiltration and/or offensives. They were aware that four VPA divisions (304th, 308th, 312th, and 320th) were in positions to threaten the Delta, but did not know where blows might fall. The Delta was obviously by far the more important front, but the north-west region was also valuable; there, a puppet Thai Federation had been created centred on Lai Chau, Thai units had been raised for the CEFEO, and French-led Thai and Meo guerrillas were usefully countering Viet Minh activity.

Each side overestimated its enemy's capabilities, and Gen. Giap, advised by a Chinese military mission (CMAG), also intended to remain basically on the defensive around the Delta, while keeping its defenders busy by infiltration. Meanwhile, he was considering committing 304th Div and units from Annam to the Laotian border country. His primary objectives would be the French air-ground bases at Lai Chau and Na San; he would then push down through Laos, potentially threatening Cambodia or South Vietnam, while keeping his options open until French reactions became clear. In August 1953 the French surprised Giap by an airborne withdrawal of the Na San garrison, but in September the VPA's 148th Sept Inf Regt and part of 316th Div were nevertheless engaged in hunting down the French-led guerrillas in the border country in preparation for a campaign into Laos.

The DRV's Minister of Defence since autumn 1946, Vo Nguyen Giap held operational command of the Vietnam People's Army throughout the war. Originally relying largely on captured prewar French and Japanese weapons and Japanese instructors, after the Communist victory in China in mid-1949 the VPA benefited from weapons, supplies, and training provided by the Chinese PLA. On the basis of its widespread guerrilla organization, by mid-1951 the VPA had created in parallel a regular main force (the 'Chu Luc'), with five light-infantry divisions and a sixth planned, plus an embryo artillery formation. Throughout Vietnam, by mid-1953 the VPA could field some 125,000 regular and 75,000 full-time regional troops, in addition to many tens of thousands of part-time auxiliaries. Over large areas it enjoyed either the sincere or at least the obedient support of the population, upon which it relied for all its everyday logistics. (ullstein-bild via Getty Images)

A large French post between Hanoi and the port of Haiphong in the Red River Delta. Two-thirds of the rural Delta was dominated by the Viet Minh; the majority of French troops there were tied down in dispersed garrisons, or as mobile reserves which had to mount repeated operations against local VPA regional and rotated-in regular units. This low-intensity war in the Delta was the constant background to the *Chu Luc*'s operations elsewhere, and any diversion of French reserves into or out of the Delta was quickly exploited. (Howard Sochurek/ The LIFE Picture Collection via Getty Images)

In order to protect the southern Delta, in October–November 1953 the French launched Operation *Mouette*, a major thrust out of its southern defences, which pinned and badly mauled the VPA 320th Div. This made Giap hesitant to move his other divisions away from the Delta approaches, but on 15 November he did order the rest of 316th Div from its Than Hoa base areas up into the Thai Highlands. At a command conference which opened on 19 November, Giap was considering sending the 308th and perhaps the 304th Divs to follow them, when news arrived of yet another unexpected development.

General Navarre had also been planning a rebalancing of effort in the Thai Highlands, to stand in the way of another thrust into Laos. For topographical reasons Lai Chau was indefensible, so it was decided to transfer (Operation *Pollux*) its garrison to a new air-ground base some 45 miles to the south. This was to be created following the airborne recapture (Operation *Castor*) of a lost former regional centre with a repairable airstrip capable of taking C-47 Dakota transports: Dien Bien Phu, on *Route Provinciale* (RP) 41 in the valley of the Nam Yum River. *Castor* was achieved easily on 20–21 November 1953, and Dien Bien Phu's garrison was soon designated Operational Group North-West (*Groupement Opérationnel du Nord-Ouest* – GONO).

OPERATIONAL BACKGROUND: THE 'PREPARED BATTLEFIELD'

GONO's operational purpose is discussed below under *Opposing Plans*, but the core concept was its ability to defend itself. At Dien Bien Phu the French tried to 'prepare a battlefield', on which they believed that the VPA could be smashed by the hammer of artillery and air support on the anvil of a ring of dug-in 'centres of resistance' (*centres de résistance* – CRs) around the airstrip – as had been achieved at Na San in December 1952.

Topography
The valley is approximately 11 miles north to south by 3 miles wide, between flanking ranges rising to some 2,300 feet. Its north–south axis is the sinuous Nam Yum River, about 30 yards wide. This was closely flanked on the east by the dirt road RP41, hooking in at the north-east corner from the direction of Tuan Giao some 40 miles away. West of the river, the rough Pavie Track

OPPOSITE
This 1:25,000-scale map was issued by the Cartographic Service of French Land Forces Far East in January 1954, with a printed disclaimer for its 'empirical' nature and undoubted errors. It includes some spot heights and 'fishbone' indications of ridges and spurs, but few contours. The consequent difficulties faced by the French artillery at Dien Bien Phu in preparing fire plans may be imagined. Denied any better maps, throughout the battle GONO (the Dien Bien Phu garrison) and GATAC/Nord (the French tactical Air Force command in Tonkin) had to rely upon mosaics of aerial photos. (Author's collection, courtesy Oliver Barnham)

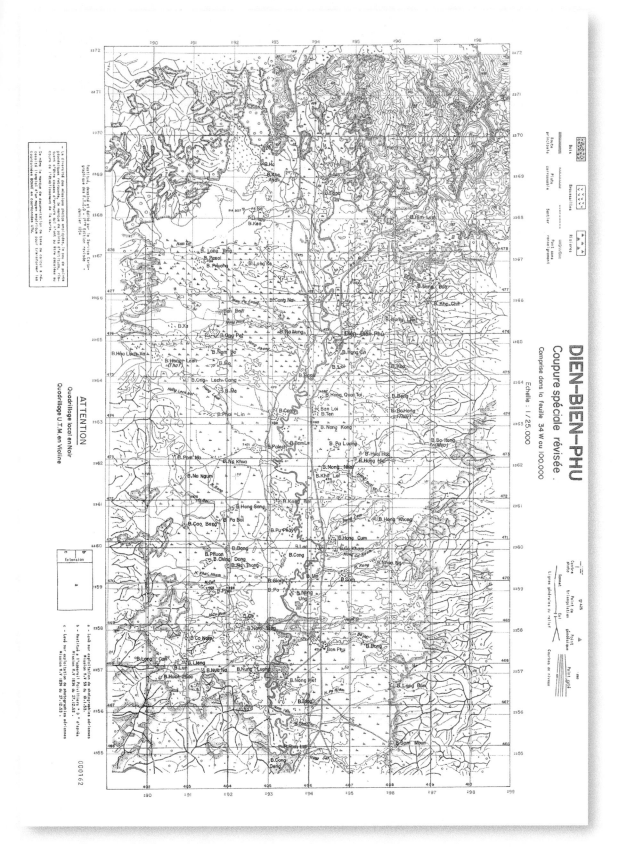

DIEN-BIEN-PHU

Coupure spéciale révisée.

Comprise dans la feuille 34 W au 100.000

Echelle : 1 / 25.000

7

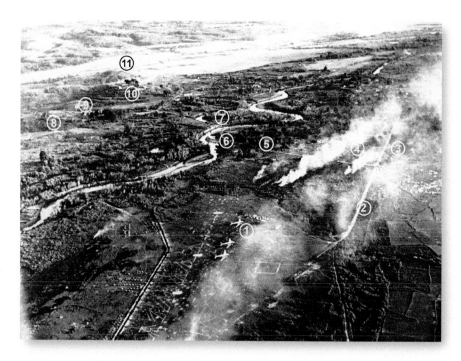

Aerial view of central site of Dien Bien Phu before its development, perhaps in the first week of December 1953, with smoke rising from trash fires. It is evidently taken from about 2,000ft altitude, looking roughly south-east from above the southern end of the airstrip (1); left of the parked C-47s, note 'dog-leg' of Japanese drainage ditch down the east side of the runway, which would become important during the fighting in April 1954. After the trees and scrub had been cleared, future positions on both sides of the Pavie Track (2) would include: (3) 155mm gunpits; (4) 105mm gunpits; (5) headquarters area, on site of demolished Muong Thanh village (here hidden by trees); (6) the original wooden bridge here would be supplemented by a Bailey bridge, just out of the photo to the left, to take the weight of tanks and loaded trucks; (7) the ox-bow 'horseshoe' of the Nam Yum; (8) Eliane 1, and (9) Eliane 4 – note generally unimpressive height of the eastern hills; (10) the slightly higher Eliane 2, with buildings that would soon be demolished, and with 'Baldy' immediately above; and (11), valley beyond the 'Five Hills' that would provide assembly areas for VPA. (Keystone France/Gamma-Rapho via Getty Images)

entered the valley's northern end from the direction of Lai Chau, about 45 miles to the north.

About one-third of the way down the valley, the original Black Thai township of Muong Thanh straddled the river. The valley had been the 'main frontier administrative centre' *(Dien Bien Phu)* of a prosperous rice- and opium-growing district encompassing scores of scattered hamlets. The valley floor was covered with their paddy-fields, broken up by streams, treelines, and large areas of scrubland. About half a mile north-west of Muong Thanh, on the west bank, lay the southern end of the 1,300-yard airstrip, oriented roughly south-east/north-west.

At Na San, success had been achieved by establishing an outer perimeter of hill positions surrounding a continuous wired and mined inner perimeter embracing entrenched strongpoints around the airstrip, from which infantry with artillery and air support mounted rapid counter-attacks to retake any lost hilltops (from opponents who lacked field artillery). At Dien Bien Phu the infantry garrison would be only slightly larger, but the ground was significantly different. There were close-in hills only on the east, with other potential sites for outworks at much greater distances from the heart of the camp. At Dien Bien Phu the airstrip pierced, rather than being surrounded by, this incomplete ring of natural defensive features, and construction of a continuous inner perimeter was never feasible.

The size of the defended perimeter obviously depended upon a compromise between the optimum distances from the core of the camp – the airfield, artillery, command headquarters, stores, ammo and fuel dumps, hospital, and positions for the 'reserve' units tasked with counter-attacks – and the number of available defenders. To occupy all the valley's surrounding heights would have taken 50 battalions, but GONO would have only 12. To the west and south, a series of entrenchments and weapon bunkers would surround the central camp, with advanced positions thrown out on the flats to the west. To the north-west, north and north-east, theoretically

The 'prepared battlefield', 13 March 1954

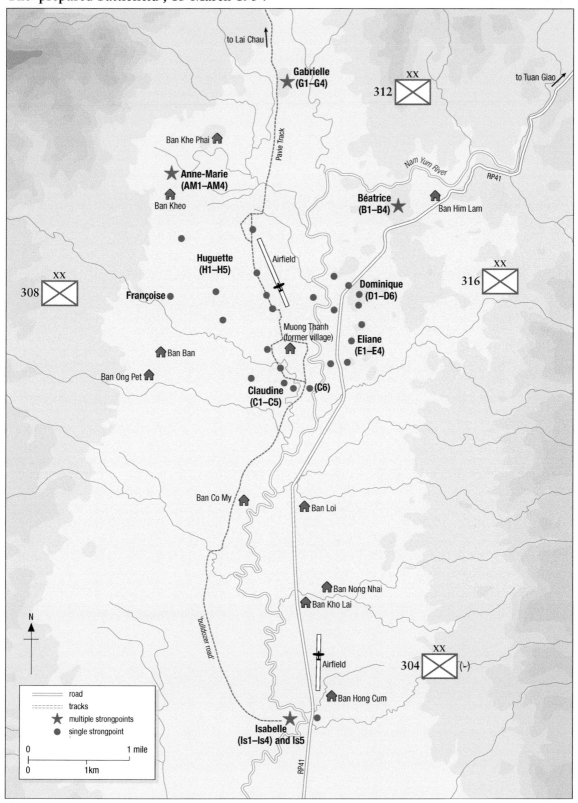

to Lai Chau

Gabrielle (G1–G4)

312

to Tuan Giao

Ban Khe Phai

Pavie Track

Anne-Marie (AM1–AM4)

Ban Kheo

Nam Yum River

RP41

Béatrice (B1–B4)

Ban Him Lam

Airfield

Huguette (H1–H5)

308

Françoise

Dominique (D1–D6)

316

Muong Thanh (former village)

Eliane (E1–E4)

Ban Ban

Ban Ong Pet

Claudine (C1–C5)

(C6)

Ban Co My

Ban Loi

N

Ban Nong Nhai

Ban Kho Lai

Airfield

304

(-)

Ban Hong Cum

road
tracks
★ multiple strongpoints
● single strongpoint

Isabelle (Is1–Is4) and Is5

0 _____ 1 mile
0 _____ 1km

RP41

9

protecting the runway, a number of isolated and very advanced positions were established beyond it and up RP41 (while still leaving a dangerous gap east of the runway).

Down the eastern face of the camp, a series of low hills mostly between 60 feet and 130 feet high rose only some 450 yards from the riverbank. It was obviously vital to incorporate these into the defended perimeter, but GONO only had the resources to patrol and place observation posts (OPs) on two neighbouring features (nicknamed 'Phoney' and 'Baldy').

Central camp

After its recapture in Operation *Castor* the village and its trees were quickly demolished for their precious timber, and during the following three months the west bank became the site of Dien Bien Phu's central camp. One of two north–south 'streets' more-or-less continued the Pavie Track in the west, and the other followed the riverbank in the east. From north to south and west to east, the component areas were occupied roughly as follows (see page 73):

- Initial lightly dug-in position of reserve unit 8 BPC.
- Stores depots; workshop areas; aircraft dispersal pens.
- About half the artillery and heavy mortars; depots; dugout hospital (after 14 April, hospital extension W of track).
- Protected dugout HQs of GM 9 and GONO, plus hull-down tank positions; HQ of GAP 2.
- Initial lightly dug-in position of reserve unit 1 BEP; compounds for *c*. 2,400 PIM (interned military prisoner) labourers.
- Ammo dumps.

'Centres of resistance'

The CRs were established gradually during December 1953–February 1954. They were given female codenames in alphabetical order, each consisting of

Operation *Castor*, 20 November 1953: on DZ 'Natacha', a squad light machine-gunner of 6 BPC mans his FM 24/29. The first two-battalion lift of GAP 1 (Airborne Group 1) was badly scattered, and the DZ was 'hotter' than had been expected: Dien Bien Phu was occupied by a VPA battalion-and-a-half, including heavy weapons. With para battalions dropped both north and south of them, and under attack by French aircraft, most of these defenders managed to slip away after putting up a stiff fight for Muong Thanh village. They left some 120 casualties, against 15 French killed and 47 wounded or injured. (ullstein-bild via Getty Images).

On the late afternoon of 20 November, scattered paras straggled in from the DZs to regroup. From their white scarves, these Vietnamese appear to be from Lt. de Wilde's 4/6 BPC, who had been misdropped as far north as Doc Lap Hill – the future CR Gabrielle. (TopFoto)

several numbered company 'strongpoints' sited for mutual support, within their own perimeters.

Like the central camp, mapping these is notoriously difficult. They were built piecemeal rather than following a truly unified plan; GONO's own maps were inadequate, and they even confused FTNV Hanoi during the battle. In some CRs there were no hard-and-fast perimeters of trenches and wire – layouts evolved throughout the battle, confusing the interpretation of such aerial photos as are available.[2] In this book we have tried to follow the valuable new research by Boylan and Olivier, but we do not pretend to offer more than approximations on the maps. The CRs and strongpoints, and the main reserve positions behind them to accomodate reinforcements, were placed as follows; their VPA designations, where known, are in [square parentheses]. All distances, (abbreviated) compass directions and heights are approximate:

Advanced northern positions, clockwise from '11 o'clock' across to '1 o'clock':

- 1 mile NW from north end of airstrip, on 90ft feature N of Ban Kheo village, strongpoints Anne-Marie 1 and 2 [Pts 104B and 104A].
- 800 yards due W from north end of airstrip, strongpoint Anne-Marie 4 [Pt 106] (became Huguette 7 from 17 March).
- At north end of airstrip, strongpoint Anne-Marie 3 [Pt 105] (became Huguette 6 from 17 March).
- On Pavie Track, 2,200 yards roughly N from north end of airstrip, CR Gabrielle, with company strongpoints within continuous perimeter on 180-foot hill [Doc Lap].
- On RP41, 2,300 yards NE from south end of airstrip, CR Béatrice, with company strongpoints on three features of 60-foot hill [Bin Lam].

Clockwise from '2 o'clock' down to '6 o'clock':
West bank:
- 350 yards E of S end of airstrip, two 105mm battery positions at Dominique 4 [Pt 203] (from third week March, in arc at S end of this, also CR Épervier [Pt 204], second position of 8 BPC).

---

2   Famously, in January 1954 GONO reported construction of a long, continuous 'wavebreaker' wire belt outside the western face of the main camp, but this appears neither in aerial photos nor in any Vietnamese source.

East bank:
- 1,100 yards NNE of S end of airstrip, between river and RP41 on 130-foot hill, strongpoint Dominique 1 [Hill E1].
- 200 yards SE of Dominique 1, on RP41, outpost Dominique 6.
- 550 yards SE of Dominique 1, E of RP41, strongpoint Dominique 2 on highest 230-foot hill [Hill D1].
- 250 yards S of Dominique 2, on an extended knee of that hill, strongpoint Dominique 5 [Hill D3].
- On flats between river and RP41, W from Dominique 5, defended 105mm battery position Dominique 3 [Pts 210, 505, and 505A].
- 550 yards S from Dominique 2, 60-foot hill strongpoint Eliane 1 [Hill C1].
- 270 yards SW from Eliane 1, 50-foot hill strongpoint Eliane 4 [Hill C2, 'Saddleback'].
- On riverside flats W of Eliane 4 and of RP41, reserve positions Eliane 12 [Pt 507] and Eliane 10 [Pt 506].
- On riverbank SW from Eliane 4, NW of 'ox-bow', reserve position Eliane 11 [Pt 509].
- 500 yards S from Eliane 4, 130-foot hill strongpoint Eliane 2 [Hill A1], site of former brick buildings.
- 500 yards NE from Eliane 2 and slightly higher, unoccupied 'Mont Fictif' ('Phoney', [Hill F]).
- 300 yards ESE from Eliane 2 and slightly lower, unoccupied but initially patrolled 'Mont Chauve' ('Baldy' [Burnt Hill]).
- Between river and RP41, W from Eliane 2, sprawling reserve area Eliane 3 [Pt A3].
- At S tip of camp, strongpoint Claudine 6 (from third week March, became CR Junon [VPA designation Pt 322], second position of 1 BEP).
- Finally, some 3½ miles S from the main camp, in a bend of the Nam Yum W of Ban Hong Cum village – reached by RP41 east of the river, and a 'bulldozer road' west of it – the completely isolated CR Isabelle guarded a dirt auxiliary airstrip (which was virtually never used). Much more important were two 105mm batteries which could cover the enemy's eastern approaches to the Elianes and Dominiques, plus a tank platoon and two infantry battalions which could (theoretically) come up to support the southern Elianes and Claudines. About half-way down RP41 to Isabelle a small post named Marcelle was initially occupied, but was abandoned probably in mid-January.

Clockwise from '7 o'clock' up to '10 o'clock':
- Inner, strongpoint Claudine 3.
- Advanced, strongpoint Claudine 5 [Pt 310]; outer, Claudine 4; inner, Claudine 2.
- Inner, strongpoint Claudine 7 [Pt 307] (became Liliane 1 from second week of April), protecting base position of 120mm mortars W of Pavie Track.
- Inner, strongpoint Claudine 1 [Pt 309] (became Lili 2 from second week of April), protecting adjacent 155mm battery W of Pavie Track, and 105mm battery(ies) E of track.
- Advanced, strongpoint Huguette 4 [Pt 311B] (became Lili 3 from second week of April); inner, on W side of Pavie Track, Huguette 3 [Pt 309A].

- Far advanced, outpost Françoise [Pt 311]; advanced, strongpoint Huguette 5 [Pt 311A]; inner, N of Huguette 3, strongpoint Huguette 2 [Pt 208].
- 100 yards W of and about halfway up airstrip, strongpoint Huguette 1[Pt 206].
- Immediately E of airstrip opposite Huguette 1, strongpoint Opéra (18–24 April only).
- SE of Opéra, in drainage ditch down E side of airstrip, 'nameless strongpoint' (from 24/25 April only).

Failures of fortification

For lack of materials and man-hours, the majority of 'strongpoints' were only fairly sketchy field fortifications. Suitable local timber was in short supply, as were the hands needed to cut it and trucks to carry it in, and later-arriving battalions found little material left. There was no local source of stone, and no provision for pouring concrete. Only on Eliane 2 were there pre-existing brick buildings, whose cellars were turned into strong dugouts, and whose rubble was recycled to make the vital 'bursting layer' in overhead cover from artillery.

The background to the consolidation of GONO and the battle that followed was a chronic shortage of available air-transport capacity. It was estimated that to lift engineer materials to Dien Bien Phu in sufficient quantity (calculated as 36,600 tons for the CRs alone, in addition to all the central facilities) would anyway have required the fantasy of a five-month airlift by the entire Indochina transport fleet. In the event, only some 4,000 tons of cargo were delivered, of which just 168 tons were actual building materials. Pierced steel plates (PSPs) for surfacing the runway accounted for 510 tons, a prefabricated Bailey bridge for another 44 tons, and about half a million empty sandbags for 160 tons, and only a wholly inadequate 3,000 tons of barbed wire were delivered.

Until now, the CEFEO had never faced artillery other than small numbers of obsolete Japanese 75mm mountain guns. By early January 1954 the high

Légionnaires at their ease in a lightly dug-in position in the west of the central camp, probably late in December 1953. Over three months, the west bank of the Nam Yum became crowded with tents, sandbag-and-bamboo shacks, shelter trenches, dugouts, gunpits and vehicle scrapes, workshop areas, power-generating and water-purification plants, and dumps for all kinds of stores, criss-crossed with tracks, telephone wires, and fairly random barbed wire. (Ernst Haas/Getty Images).

Amid typical 'High Region' scenery, paras salute their buried dead on Hill 1175, during the failed sortie to the north on 11–15 December 1953 to rescue retreating Lai Chau survivors at Muong Pon village. 1 BEP and 5 BPVN needed artillery support to fight their way out of the valley of Dien Bien Phu on the 11th, and another 400 rounds, plus a B-26 napalm strike, to get back into it on the 15th. The two battalions lost a total of 47 dead and missing and had 69 wounded during the operation. This costly failure suggested, within three weeks of *Castor*, that GONO's anticipated external operations were an illusion. (Hulton Archive via Getty Images)

command was aware of the movement south by VPA 105mm howitzers; the implications were understood by GONO leaders with World War II experience, but not by many of their subordinates. But the means to protect dugouts with at least 3 feet of rammed earth between two layers of heavy, strongly propped logs, all under a hard 'bursting layer', simply did not exist at Dien Bien Phu.

Nor did the expertise or the man-hours to construct such defences: the small engineer unit (just 326 strong) was needed for specialist tasks, and the infantry, ordered to build their own positions, were distracted during December 1953–February 1954 by simultaneous orders to send out fighting sorties in up to multi-battalion strength. In consequence of all these factors, when the blow fell on 13 March 1954 many positions were very far from shell- or even mortar-proof.

Moreover, for lack of means to extend perimeters to true 'military crests' dominating the slopes, some hill strongpoints were poorly designed for defence. Individual trenches branched out from their perimeters seeking better fields of fire, but these also offered assault troops easy routes inwards.

Failure of sorties

VPA elements arrived in the hills around the camp sooner and in greater strength than anticipated. Between 23 November 1953 and 16 February 1954 ten main external operations were carried out by para and infantry units, usually with artillery and air support and sometimes with tanks (see *Chronology*). Those to cover the installation of CRs Béatrice and Gabrielle were successful; those to link up with the retreating garrison of Lai Chau failed, and contacts with pro-French guerrillas were limited; and later thrusts by several battalions at a time, attempting to locate and destroy VPA positions, achieved nothing lasting, and had to fight hard to get back into the camp.

By 17 February 1954, GONO casualties since 20 November 1953 had reached 1,000, and sorties were thereafter limited to local tactical patrols. (However, these would continue until late in the battle, particularly by Legion units west and south-west of the main camp, where large areas of the valley remained unoccupied by the VPA.)

CHRONOLOGY

Note: In the context of VPA attacks, 'part(s)' of a regiment indicate battalion- or two-battalion strength. In the context of French defence or counter-attack, it usually indicates two- or even one-company strength. During April–May 1954, French reaction/reinforcement forces for the CRs dwindled into scratch battle-groups assembled from companies or even platoons, sometimes from different decimated units.

In the below chronology, entries in **bold** type and bracketed indicate important 'background' events; and those in *italic* type indicate continuing situations, rather than single events.

Occupation

1953

15 November	Operation *Pollux* (withdrawal of Lai Chau garrison) begins; first column of Thai auxiliaries leaves overland for Dien Bien Phu.
20 November	Operation *Castor* (occupation of Dien Bien Phu) by GAP 1 begins: 6 BPC, II/1 RCP, 1 BPC, part of 35 RALP (75mm RCLs), and medical 1 ACP air-dropped, commanded by Brig.-Gen. Jean Gilles. Occupying VPA 910th Bn/148th Sept Inf Regt plus companies from 48th Regt/320th Div withdraw after initial resistance.
21 November	Reinforcement by GAP 2 begins: 1 BEP, 8 BPC and 1 CEPML air-dropped.
22 November	5 BPVN air-dropped.
23 November	First exploratory sorties by 6 BPC and II/1 RCP.
24 November	First *c.* 700 Thai auxiliaries arrive from Lai Chau.
25 November	Dien Bien Phu airstrip open to C-47s. First two 105mm howitzers flown in, to be joined by second section on **29th.**
1 December	First six F8F Bearcats arrive for local support missions.
(3 December	**Gen. Navarre decides to accept battle at Dien Bien Phu.**)
4 December	Major sorties by 8 BPC and 1 BPC; Maj.-Gen. Cogny orders installation of CR Béatrice. First engineers of 31 BG arrive.
5–11 December	Regular units of Lai Chau garrison flown out. Approximately 2,140 French-led Thai auxiliaries leave overland for Dien Bien Phu; only 288 will survive pursuit and ambushes by 316th Div.
(6 December	**Communist government of DRV decides on general mobilization of personnel and resources throughout country, to support planned Dien Bien Phu operation.**)
6–10 December	III/10 RAC (105mm) flown in.
6–12 December	Progressive withdrawal of GAP 1.
7 December	Col. Christian de Castries flown in to take over command from Brig.-Gen. Gilles. 1 BEP, 6 and 8 BPC cover installation of CR at Béatrice.
11–15 December	Sortie by 1 BEP and 5 BPVN to rescue Lai Chau survivors fails, despite air and artillery cover – *c.* 110 para casualties.
c. 17 December	316th Div completes arrival east of Dien Bien Phu.
18 December	First disassembled M24 tanks arrive.
By 20 December	Arrival of GM 9: I/ and III/13 DBLE, III/3 RTA.
21 December	Medical 1 ACP replaced by 29 ACM.

21–25 December Public-relations exercise Operation *Régate*: on Gen. Navarre's orders, GAP 2 march south to Sop Nao to link with northwards column from Laos, then return.

22 December Last few Thai survivors from Lai Chau arrive.

26 December Withdrawal of 5 BPVN.

27 December Withdrawal of 35 RALP element.

By 31 December Arrival of GM 6: II/1 RTA, V/7 RTA, III/3 REI; plus 11/IV/4 RAC (155mm), and half of II/4 RAC (105mm).

308th Div is arriving north of Dien Bien Phu.

1954

(1 January **Gen. Navarre reports movement of VPA 37mm AA guns towards Dien Bien Phu.)**

(6 January **Maj.-Gen. Cogny reports movement of VPA 105mm howitzers towards Dien Bien Phu.)**

During January *Arrival of I/2 REI and I/4 RTM; construction of CR Gabrielle.*

6–8 January Failed sortie by 8 BPC.

12 January 1 BEP sortie east of Isabelle – 38 casualties.

14 January Remainder of II/4 RAC flown in.

15 January 312th Div is arriving north-east of Dien Bien Phu; Gen. Giap arrives at Dien Bien Phu forward HQ.

20 January Tank squadron operational.

(20 January **French Operation *Atlante* begins on coast of Annam.)**

c. **24 January** 304th Div is arriving south-east of Dien Bien Phu.

(26 January **Gen. Giap postpones planned late-January assaults in favour of prolonged siege.** *Artillery to be re-installed in improved positions; new major programme of road- and path-building and entrenchment ordered.)*

27 January 308th Div, plus part of 176th Regt/316th Div and 148th Sept Inf Regt leave siege army for diversionary thrust south into Laos.

31 January Failed sortie north by 1 BEP, 8 BPC, parts of III/13 DBLE and BT 2.

1 February First VPA 75mm artillery ranging shots fall on camp.

3 February 30-minute VPA bombardment. *(From this date on, ranging and harassing 75mm fire – but not 105mm? – almost daily.)*

6–7 February Major sortie east from Dominique and Béatrice by parts of 1 BEP, 8 BPC, I/4 RTM and BT 2; heavily engaged by dug-in enemy – 90-plus casualties.

9 February Sortie west from Huguette by parts of I/13 DBLE, I/2 REI, I/4 RTM and BT 2 – 28 casualties.

12–16 February Largest and final sortie operations: west of Anne-Marie by BT 3; north of Gabrielle, and north and south-east of Béatrice, by parts of V/7 RTA and III/13 DBLE, III/3 RTA, III/3 REI, and 1 BEP and 8 BPC, with tank, artillery, and air support. Prolonged fighting against dug-in and counter-attacking enemy – 114 casualties.

17 February Maj.-Gen. Cogny orders cessation of major sortie operations.

18 February Inspection by Surgeon General Gaston Jeansotte reports medical facilities at Dien Bien Phu wholly inadequate. ACM 44 flown in subsequently.

**(Announcement at four-power Berlin talks – between USSR, US, France, and

UK – of Geneva Conference, including China, to begin on 26 April. *Victory at Dien Bien Phu thus assumes major political importance for both sides.*)

21 February — 308th Div begins return march from Laos.

12 March — Col. de Castries warns unit commanders of all-out VPA assault at 1700hrs the following afternoon.

First assault phase, 13–17 March

13 March — Major VPA bombardment from *c*. 1720hrs causes significant damage and casualties in main camp and at Isabelle. GM 9 HQ destroyed, Lt.-Col. Jules Gaucher mortally wounded.

F8F Bearcat shot down; resupply flights into camp cease, replaced by air-drops, although casevac flights continue.

13/14 March — Shelling of CRs Gabrielle, and Béatrice (III/13 DBLE) 1720–1930hrs is followed by diversionary attacks on former, and all-out infantry assaults on latter by 141st and 209th Regts. Béatrice falls by 0230hrs.

14 March — No counter-attack on Béatrice is attempted. 5 BPVN is air-dropped in; last serviceable F8Fs fly out.

14/15 March — Intermittent bombardment and infantry probing of CR Gabrielle (V/7 RTA) from 1830hrs. Barrage proper begins at 0330hrs, preparing renewed assaults by parts of 165th and 88th Regts, which make steady progress.

0515–0545hrs, Lt.-Col. Pierre Langlais orders sortie to Gabrielle by part of 1 BEP, 5 BPVN, and tanks. 1 BEP and tanks fight past resistance at Ban Khe Phai, but part of 5 BPVN hesitates. Due to failures of command-and-control and communication, the mission achieves only extraction of survivors; Gabrielle falls by 0900hrs.

15 March — GONO artillery commander Col. Charles Piroth commits suicide.

Air Force F8F and Navy F6F shot down.

15–17 March — Desertions from BT 3 companies in CR Anne-Marie; Anne-Marie 1 and 2 abandoned; Anne-Marie 3 and 4 renamed Huguette 6 and 7. Medical 6 ACP air-dropped.

16 March — 6 BPC air-dropped, plus medical 3 ACP, replacements for casualties, and two replacement 105s.

The lull: 17–30 March

Giap concentrates on siege entrenchment around all French perimeters, while re-siting artillery, replenishing ammo, and incorporating first casualty replacements.

While continuing to mount patrols and trench raids, GONO concentrates on resupply, consolidating defences, and night casevac flights. New defensive locations created: Épervier, S of airstrip (for 8 BPC); Junon, ex-Claudine 6 at S of camp (for 1 BEP); and Dominique 6, on RP41 (for part of 5 BPVN).

19 March — Col. de Castries' pessimistic report gives Maj.-Gen. Cogny an excuse not to drop requested II/1 RCP.

21 March — Legion road-opening sortie to CR Isabelle needs two tank platoons to break through block around Ban Kho Lai and Ban Nong Nhai.

22 March — 1 BEP and two tank platoons from Claudine, plus infantry and tank platoon from Isabelle, take 5 hours to break through VPA trenches cutting RP41.

Loss of an H-19 helicopter to shellfire halts attempts to casevac by this means.

24–31 March	*During week, three Dakotas shot down over camp, plus one forced down at Isabelle and destroyed by shellfire. From 27 March, Air Force ceases air-drops below 6,500 feet, with consequent scattering.*
24 March	Alleged 'putsch of paratroop mafia'. Col. de Castries confirms Lt.-Col. Langlais as chief of operations (see *Opposing Commanders*).
24–29 March	Paras and tanks fight several engagements on Isabelle road; near Eliane 4 and Dominique 1; and (with BT 2) north of Huguettes 6 and 7.
28 March	Major sortie against AA guns at Bang Ong Pet and Ban Ban west of Claudine, by 6 and 8 BPC plus tanks (see battlescene on pages 54–55); 110 para casualties.
	(Airfield finally closed.)
29 March	First significant rainfall; *thereafter intermittent until 25 April.*
30 March	GONO abandons attempts to keep road open to Isabelle.

Second assault phase, 30 March–5 April: 'Battle of the Five Hills'

30/31 March	VPA bombardment *c.* 1715–1830hrs. Eliane 1 (part of I/4 RTM) captured before 1925hrs by part of 98th Regt. Dominique 1 (parts of III/3 RTA and 5 BPVN) falls by 1945hrs to parts of 141st Regt. Dominique 2 (half of III/3 RTA and a CSM) taken before 2000hrs by parts of 209th Regt.
	With artillery and tank support, Dominique 5 (part of BT 2), Dominique 3 (parts of II/4 RAC and III/3 RTA – see battlescene on pages 60–61), Eliane 2 (parts of I/4 RTM, I/13 DBLE, and 1 BEP), and Eliane 4 (part of 5 BPVN) are successfully defended. Diversionary attacks on

	Huguette 7 (part of 5 BPVN) and Isabelle 5 (Group Wieme – Thai auxiliaries) are also driven off.
31 March	Attempts to secure DZ for anticipated (but aborted) drop of II/1 RCP, and to recapture Elaine 1 and Dominique 2, all fail. Dominique 5 abandoned.
	Navy SB2C Helldiver shot down.
31 March/1 April	Eliane 2 (parts of I/4 RTM, I/13 DBLE, 6 and 8 BPC, plus tanks) is held against attacks by parts of 102nd and 174th Regts. Huguette 7 (part of 5 BPVN) holds off part of 36th Regt.
1/2 April	Eliane 2 (1 BEP, parts of 6 BPC and I/2 REI) repels attacks by parts of 102nd and 174th Regts. Huguette 7 (part of I/2 REI) is captured by parts of 36th Regt. Part of II/1 RCP is air-dropped.
2 April	Attempt to retake Huguette 7 (part of 5 BPVN, plus tanks) is aborted. Thai auxiliaries desert from outpost Françoise.
2/3 April	Eliane 2 (1 BEP) repels attacks by parts of 102nd Regt. Probing attacks on Dominique 3 (part of III/3 RTA), on Huguette 6 (parts of I/2 REI and III/13 DBLE), and on Isabelle 5 (Group Wieme, part of II/1 RTA) are all repelled. Françoise abandoned.
3/4 April	Counter-attack by part of 6 BPC plus tanks heavily defeats 165th Regt's assault on Huguette 6. Part of II/1 RCP is air-dropped.
4/5 April	Huguette 6 captured by parts of 165th and 141st Regts. Counter-attack by part of 8 BPC plus tanks fails, but another by part of II/1 RCP retakes position – *c.* 220 para casualties. End of second assault phase.
5 April	All four M45 .50-cal. quadmounts reunited in Épervier.

5/6 April	Remainder of II/1 RCP is air-dropped, plus first non-para volunteers.
6 April	Legion patrol recovers two misdropped 75mm RCLs of 35 RALP.
7 April	Resupply drops now limited to 8,500 feet-plus, with consequent bad scattering. Some Thai auxiliary companies and 12/BT 3 disarmed and disbanded.

Stranglehold and attrition: 8–30 April

	Continuous VPA extension of encirclement and approach trenches around remaining French positions; intermittent shelling, and tightening of AA cordon. French units respond with increasingly costly sorties by infantry and tanks to destroy trenches, and to resupply Huguettes 1 and 6, which are becoming surrounded by units from 308th and 312th Divs.
8 April	I/4 RTM begins establishing new Liliane strongpoints on western perimeter: Liliane 3 (ex-Huguette 4), and Liliane 2 and 1 (ex-Claudine 1 and 2).
9 April	Navy SB2C Helldiver shot down.
9/10 April	Half of 2 BEP is air-dropped.
10 April	6 BPC retakes Eliane 1 from part of 174th Regt, and is then relieved by half of II/1 RCP.
10/11 April	Parts of II/1 RCP, 1 BEP and 5 BPVN hold off attacks on Eliane 1 by parts of 174th and 88th Regts – *c.* 200 para casualties.
11/12 April	Attacks on Eliane 1 by parts of 98th and 209th Regts repelled with difficulty by parts of II/1 RCP, 1 BEP, and 5 BPVN – *c.* 130 para casualties. 2 BEP parachute insertion completed.
12–13 April	Air Force B-26 and two F8F Bearcats bomb camp in error; Navy PB4Y Privateer shot down; five C-119s

	misdrop hundreds of 105mm shells to VPA. Medical 5 ACP is air-dropped.
14 April	First VPA trench dug across runway.
14–18 April	Parts of 6 and 8 BPC, 1 and 2 BEP, plus tanks, are heavily engaged during successive night resupply missions to Huguette 1 and 6.
18 April	Huguette 6 abandoned; I/2 REI and 5 BPVN survivors join composite company in new strongpoint Opéra opposite Huguette 1.
18–19 April	Major operation needed to enable parts of I/13 DBLE to relieve parts of I/2 REI in Huguettes 1, 2, and 3.
20/21 and 21/22 April	
	Parts of II/1 RCP and 6 BPC successfully raid VPA-held Dominique 6 and 5 respectively. On same two nights, resupply attempts fail to reach Huguette 1.
22/23 April	36th Regt penetrates Huguette 1 perimeter through infiltration tunnels, taking strongpoint by 0300hrs. Trenches blocking French access from Huguette 2 are reinforced by 88th Regt.
23 April	2 BEP's attempts to retake Huguette 1 via Opéra and Huguette 2 fail – 95 para casualties.
	Navy F6F Hellcat shot down.
24 April	1 and 2 BEPs merged into Foreign Parachute Marching Battalion (BMEP), under the former's Maj. Guiraud. Strongpoint Opéra abandoned, replaced by 'nameless strongpoint' further south-east.
25 April	Heavy monsoon rains begin. *From now on, waterlogged trenches will be flooded anything up to waist deep, and parapets collapse; tanks often bog down; and all movement for both sides is slow and difficult.*

26 April	Two Air Force B-26s and one Navy F6F Hellcat shot down.
	(Geneva Conference begins.)
29 April	Garrison put on half-rations.

Third assault phase: 30 April–6 May

30 April/1 May	Huguette 5 (parts of BMEP and I/2 REI) repels attack by part of 88th Regt.
1/2 May	Bombardment of all positions *c.* 1630–1930hrs. At/by *c.* 0200hrs, three strongpoints are lost: Huguette 5 (part of BMEP) to parts of 88th Regt; Eliane 1 (II/1 RCP) to parts of 98th and 176th Regts (see battlescene on pages 74–75); and Dominique 3 (parts of 6 BPC and BT 2) to parts of 209th Regt. Isabelle 5 is captured by part of 57th Regt at *c.* 0345hrs. Eliane 2 (parts of I and III/13 DBLE) and Eliane 4 (part of 5 BPVN) are assaulted by parts of 174th and 98th Regts respectively, and Liliane 3 (part of I/4 RTM) by part of 36th Regt, but all hold out. French casualties during night are *c.* 490.
2 May	Counter-attack (parts of III/3 REI and II/1 RTA plus tanks) recaptures Isabelle 5 by 1600hrs, but only OP re-installed.
2/3 May	Part of 1 BPC is air-dropped.
3/4 May	Liliane 3 (1/I/4 RTM) is attacked via infiltration tunnels by parts of 36th Regt, and falls 0335hrs; counter-attack (part of I/13 DBLE) fails – the night costs 222 French casualties. Part of 1 BPC is air-dropped.
5/6 May	Part of 1 BPC is air-dropped; unit will remain incomplete.
6 May	C-119 Packet shot down. From 1510hrs, focused bombardments of Elianes 2 and 4 and Claudine 5, and by MRLs on artillery positions.

Final assaults: 6–7 May

6/7 May	Parts of 102nd Regt assault Claudine 5 (parts of I/2 REI and III/13 DBLE) at 2100hrs, capturing it at 0230hrs. Mine dug under Eliane 2 (1 BPC) is detonated at 2030hrs, but effect limited; delayed assaults by parts of 174th Regt; attempts to reinforce by scratch companies from BMEP fail; position overrun at 0440hrs. Eliane 4 (remnants of II/1 RCP, 5 BPVN, 1 BPC, BMEP and III/3 RTA) assaulted by parts of 98th Regt from 2030hrs; positions lost and retaken in see-saw fighting. Renewed VPA barrage; part of 9th Regt committed 0730hrs; hill falls at *c.* 0930hrs. From 2100hrs, on riverside flats, Eliane 12 (parts of BT 2, III/3 RTA, assorted walking wounded) repels attacks by part of 209th Regt.
7 May	Eliane 10 (parts of 6 and 8 BPC, BT 2) finally falls to parts of 165th Regt at 0930hrs. (See also Eliane 4, above.) VPA shelling continues, but there is apparently no further infantry fighting. Survivors in Eliane 3 fall back over river at 1500hrs, by which time Elianes 11 and 12 have also been abandoned. At 1630hrs, GONO HQ orders units to destroy weapons, ammo, and equipment, and to cease fire. At 1730hrs, HQ broadcasts radio message announcing unilateral ceasefire. 308th and 312th Divs make unresisted general advance into the camp.
7/8 May	Two columns from Isabelle attempt to break out southwards, but fail; Isabelle surrenders 0150hrs on 8 May. Navy Privateer shot down.

OPPOSING COMMANDERS

FRENCH

The French C-in-C Far East, **Lt.-Gen. Henri Navarre** (1896–1983), was a cavalryman with combat experience in both World Wars, and a long background in Intelligence and staff appointments. He had commanded the light-armoured 3rd Moroccan Spahis Regt in Gen. Jean de Lattre's French First Army in Alsace and Germany in 1944–45, and most recently 5th Armoured Div in Germany. Navarre was intellectually and politically astute, energetic and decisive, but coolly secretive by nature – an 'air-conditioned general'.

His subordinate Commander Land Forces North Vietnam, **Maj.-Gen. René Cogny** (1904–68), was a more approachable character. A Norman artilleryman who had risen from a humble background by academic talent, Cogny had escaped from German captivity in 1941. Later Resistance activity led to his arrest by the Gestapo in 1943, and six months of captivity and torture before being sent to a concentration camp; he walked with a limp

(Middle, left to right) Generals Gilles, Navarre, and Cogny at Dien Bien Phu shortly after *Castor*. Although he had won the battle of Na San a year previously, Jean Gilles was glad to hand over command of GONO to Col. de Castries on 7 December, being fully aware of the folly of committing airborne troops to lengthy positional fighting. Henri Navarre was described as having a 'feline' aloofness, and throughout the battle displayed the cool detachment that is perhaps necessary for a theatre commander. René Cogny called himself 'Delta Man'; he disapproved of tying down Tonkin's airborne reserve at Dien Bien Phu, and his semi-detached attitude during the battle infuriated Navarre and depressed de Castries. (ullstein-bild via Getty Images)

for the rest of his life. Posted to Vietnam in 1950, Cogny had commanded a Mobile Group in the Delta before Navarre offered him FTNV. No enthusiast for Operation *Castor*, he was entirely focused on the defence of the Delta, an attitude which contributed to an increasingly toxic relationship with Navarre. Cogny was a man of presence and charm, but he had a bad habit of confiding in journalists.

The initial para-drop on Dien Bien Phu was led by the one-eyed **Brig.-Gen. Jean Gilles** (1904–61), a *Tirailleurs Sénégalais* veteran of Morocco in the 1930s and French First Army in 1944–45. Serving on Gen. Philippe Leclerc's staff in South Vietnam in 1946, he had qualified as a paratrooper in 1949. His victory at Na San in December 1952 earned him his general's stars and the inspector-generalship of Airborne Troops Indochina, but he remained a dour realist.

His replacement as commander of GONO at Dien Bien Phu from 7 December 1953 was, like Maj.-Gen. Cogny, obliged to use a walking stick, in his case by wounds while he was leading a Mobile Group. **Colonel (later Brig.-Gen.) Christian de Castries** (1902–91) came from an aristocratic old military family.[3] He had distinguished himself by aggressive initiative in World War II, which he ended as a squadron commander in Navarre's Spahi regiment. He had been in Indochina on-and-off since 1946, first under Leclerc in Cochinchina, and later under de Lattre and Salan in the Delta, commanding first GM 2 and then GM 1 in 1951–52. Immediately before his appointment to GONO he had earned praise in joint command of GMs 2 and 3 during Operation *Mouette* in October 1953. Selected at a time when GONO was envisaged partly as a hub for external operations, de Castries was not the man for a prolonged positional defence, and he would occasionally give way to defeatism. However, he was quick to cede the necessary authority to subordinates with more appropriate experience, and he seems to have retained more agency and respect among them than some commentators have claimed.

Before late March, GONO's internal command structure appears rather unwieldy. Under Col. de Castries and his chief of staff Lt.-Col. René Keller, it was divided between Northern, Central and Southern sectors, some of whose commanders held 'superimposed' appointments. The Northern Sector (CRs Gabrielle and Anne-Marie) was initially the responsibility of Lt.-Col. André Trancart, the former commander at Lai Chau. The vital Central Sector (outpost Françoise, and CRs Huguette, Claudine, Dominique, Eliane, and Béatrice) was initially commanded by **Lt.-Col. Jules Gaucher** (1905–54) of GM 9, a tough Legion Indochina hand since before World War II, who was simultaneously regimental commander of 13 DBLE. The Southern Sector (outpost Marcelle and CR Isabelle) was the fief of **Lt.-Col. (later Col.) André Lalande** (1913–95), commander of both GM 6 and 3 REI. Originally a *Chasseur Alpin* who had taken his first wound at Narvik in 1940, Lalande was later a Legion veteran of Bir Hakeim, the Gustav Line, and Alsace.

After Gaucher's death on 13/14 March he was immediately replaced in command of the Central Sector by **Lt.-Col. (later Col) Pierre Langlais** (1909–86) of GAP 2, command of the latter then passing to Maj. (later Lt.-Col.) Hubert de Séguin-Pazzis. A ferociously hot-tempered Breton,

---

3 On 16 April 1954 many of the senior officers of the besieged garrison were promoted by one rank.

Langlais thus became GONO's de facto chief of operations, a post for which – after his early mishandling of the Gabrielle counter-attack – he proved well fitted. After prewar service with camel companies in the Sahara, Langlais had fought as an infantryman in Italy, Alsace, and Germany, and at the head of a Colonial Infantry battalion in the streets of Hanoi in late 1946; he had qualified as a paratrooper by the time he returned for his third tour in June 1953.

After the much-exaggerated 'putsch of the paratroop mafia' on 24 March, the command structure was rationalized, or rather consolidated – it is clear that newly arrived officers were prevented from interfering with the already established fighting teamwork. (Bernard Fall's account of the relevant meeting, apparently relying upon that of a resentful staff officer, seems to be over-dramatic.)

Lalande's command at Isabelle was undisturbed. The dead Col. Piroth was replaced as artillery commander by **Lt.-Col. Guy Vaillant**, and **Lt.-Col. Gaston Ducruix** replaced the evacuated Keller as GONO's chief of staff. The Northern Sector positions no longer existed, and Trancart was henceforth appointed the camp's head of personnel. The Central Sector was divided at the river into eastern and western fronts; despite the newly arrived **Lt.-Col. Maurice Lemeunier**'s command of 13 DBLE and GM 9, Langlais retained personal control of operations on the eastern face (the Dominiques and Elianes). The Claudines and Huguettes in the western face were commanded by the newcomer **Lt.-Col. Pierre Voinot**, formerly of IV/7 RTA.

In practice, Maj. de Séguin-Pazzis' operational authority over GAP 2 was partly assumed by **Maj. (later Lt.-Col.) Marcel Bigeard** (1916–2010) from 6 BPC, now appointed Langlais' deputy for planning counter-attacks, with Capt. Thomas succeeding him in command of his battalion. A sergeant in 1939, the humbly born Bigeard had earned rapid promotions and a chestful of French and British decorations (including the DSO) while serving with the Free French and the *maquis*. Now on his third Indochina tour, he knew the Thai Highlands well, and had led his crack colonial paras to a deliberately pursued fame (photographers were always welcome, provided they could keep up). This, and French Army *snobbisme,* made him unpopular with some contemporaries; but he had repeatedly demonstrated great energy and leadership, and a tactical talent for orchestrating companies in combat with map and radio.

While Bigeard retained this responsibility, from 11 April Langlais appointed 'district' commanders who reported to him at a daily conference: the Five Hills (Maj. Bréchignac, II/1 RCP); the 'low' Dominiques and Elianes (Maj. Chenel, BT 2); Épervier (Capt. Tourret, 8 BPC); the Huguettes (Maj. Guiraud, 1 BEP/BMEP); and Liliane and Claudine (Maj. Vadot, 13 DBLE).

Colonel Christian de Castries in his headquarters at Dien Bien Phu, wearing his trademark red Spahi sidecap. He was inevitably scapegoated after the fall of Dien Bien Phu, being accused of defeatist inactivity. In fact, after he passed operational command to Lt.-Col. Langlais they maintained a good relationship; De Castries was fully involved in some operational decisions, and tireless in badgering Maj.-Gen. Cogny for the men, supplies, and air support that the garrison desperately needed. His courage was never in doubt, and an illuminating detail of his record is that when he first joined the army he had served in the ranks for two years before selection for officer training. (Bettmann Archive via Getty Images)

VIETNAMESE

General Giap (third left, dark shirt) in one of his forward HQs near Dien Bien Phu. This is believed to be in the extensive cave system near Tham Phua in the Muong Phang hills which was used from the second week of January, apart from a brief period spent at Na Tau during 18–30 January. (AFP/Getty Images)

While always answerable to President Ho Chi Minh, and to the more demanding Communist Party Central Committee, **Vo Nguyen Giap** (1911?–2013) was field commander-in-chief of the VPA throughout the Indochina War. The son of a well-to-do farmer who died in French imprisonment (as did Giap's first wife), he was educated at a Catholic lycée in Hue, joined the Indochinese Communist Party in 1931, and by the time he gained a law degree in 1938 had been politically active for many years. Unable to progress in his profession for that reason, he worked as a history teacher while privately studying military history. In May 1940 he joined Ho Chi Minh in Communist-held territory in China, where he studied the strategy and tactics of Mao's People's Liberation Army. Unlike several of his subordinates, Giap is not known to have attended any formal military academy. In 1942 he returned to Tonkin to establish a clandestine intelligence network in the frontier hills, later forming the first armed platoon, and in August 1945 he led the already sizeable Vietnam Liberation Army into Hanoi. As Minister of the Interior during Ho's absence negotiating in France in 1946, Giap ruthlessly purged non-Communist nationalist elements from the previously broad-based Viet Minh organization, and created extensive concealed infrastructure in the interior of Tonkin. On Ho's return Giap was appointed Minister of Defence; after briefly resisting the French in the Delta cities when open war broke out in November–December 1946, Giap then led the *Chu Luc* 'regulars' back into the hills.

During the VPA's 1947–49 highland guerrilla phase of road ambushes and attacks on isolated posts in Tonkin, Giap presided over a steady growth in the concentration and capability of his dispersed units. He created the first multi-battalion formation (308th Bde/Div) in mid-1949, and soon afterwards Mao's victory in China brought the VPA transformative logistic and training support.

For reasons of morale, it was imperative that newly 'regularized' regional infantry be successfully blooded in the 1950–51 autumn–spring campaign season. In planning this 'Frontier Campaign' Giap was advised by a veteran Chinese military envoy, Chen Geng, who was critical of VPA performance in the early assault phase in September 1950. Giap was initially wrong-footed by the French reaction, but he immediately orchestrated a coordinated response, leading in October to decisive success along *Route Coloniale* (RC) 4, and the consequent French abandonment of Lang Son and virtually the whole of Tonkin north of the Delta.

Now with unhindered access to and from China, the formation of divisions progressed rapidly, and Giap claims to have had some 60,000 regular infantry in Tonkin early in 1951. However, he then threw away more than one-third of them in premature attempts to invade the French-held Delta. By leaving the forested hills and committing parts of four divisions on this open terrain, he presented the new French C-in-C, Gen. de Lattre, with the perfect opportunity to exploit his artillery, armour, riverine navy, and airpower. He also exposed his own lack of experience in manoeuvring large forces, or in responding intelligently to the confusing challenges of prolonged combat. Giap the amateur was simply out-generalled by a professional; in January–June 1951 three failed offensives cost him perhaps 17,000 of his main force in killed and captured alone, and exposed him to severe criticism by the Party Central Committee.

Protected by Ho Chi Minh, Giap escaped dismissal, and it was fortunate for him that in late 1951 Gen. de Lattre (who was dying of cancer) himself made an overambitious error. In November he committed most of his available manoeuvre units to recapturing Hoa Binh, some 25 miles south of the Delta's new perimeter defences. Paratroops seized the objective, but thereafter the installed garrison depended upon vulnerable links via RC6 and the Black River. Giap patiently wove a noose around the town and virtually cut it off, forcing de Lattre's acting successor Gen. Raoul Salan to make a difficult fighting withdrawal in February 1952. During this campaign Giap successfully kept three divisions supplied during three months' fighting, and they also demonstrated new capabilities with 75mm mountain guns and 12.7mm heavy AA machine guns.

With his army benefiting both from restored morale (after this success even under French-ruled skies), and from increasing Chinese supplies now that the Korean War was over, in the 1952–53 season Giap committed three divisions, with recoilless guns and heavy mortars, to a new front. The Thai Highlands around the middle Black River, some 150 miles west of the Delta, were almost roadless country with few airstrips, where the French would have difficulty bringing their greater firepower to bear. In this campaign Giap demonstrated a greatly improved ability to manoeuvre formations over long distances in difficult terrain, avoiding air observation even during a major river crossing. He also succeeded in sustaining 30,000 troops far from their bases, while they overran small French garrisons and drove the survivors before them.

He only failed in his final assault in December 1952, on a strong French force mostly airlifted into a defensible position at Na San. Giap's troops were by then tired and short of supplies, the topography was against him, and for once his scout companies failed to give him an accurate picture of his opponents. With effective tactical air support and uninterrupted aerial resupply and casevac, the French garrison of this 'air-ground base' inflicted some 3,000 VPA losses while holding off several assaults and recapturing lost ground, for only about 500 own casualties. Giap withdrew, but he again learned the lessons: such battles required true field artillery, stronger AA protection, and much greater logistic resources. In 1954 he would benefit from all of these.

Giap's chief of staff at Dien Bien Phu, **Hoang Van Thai** (1915?–1986), was a former miner who had joined the Party in 1938. He received Chinese

A stern portrait of Van Tien Dung, VPA Chief of General Staff from November 1953, photographed during the ceasefire talks after Dien Bien Phu. Escaping from French imprisonment in 1944, in August 1945 he had led the Viet Minh seizure of power in Hoa Binh, Ninh Binh, and Than Hoa provinces. He would remain in post as CGS until 1978, planning the 1972 and 1975 offensives against the Republic of Vietnam, and becoming Minister of Defence in 1980. (Bettmann Archive via Getty Images).

military training at the Liuzhou academy in 1941–43, and was one of Giap's first comrades in the hills of Tonkin. Ho Chi Minh appointed him the VPA's first Chief of General Staff in 1945, and he acted as front commander for the 1950 Frontier ('RC4') Campaign. In November 1953 he was replaced as CGS by **Van Tien Dung**, and, while retaining the post of Deputy CGS, was sent to head Giap's staff for the Dien Bien Phu campaign, with (typically of the Viet Minh) both a supportive and a supervisory role.

Surprisingly to our eyes, the divisional commanders at Dien Bien Phu were not general officers, but usually held the formal rank of colonel; their authority was essentially derived from their status within the Viet Minh's integrated politico-military hierarchy. The commander of the (only partly present) 304th Div since its formation in 1950, **Hoang Minh Thao** (1921–2008) was another graduate of Liuzhou. The elite 308th Div was commanded by **Vuong Thua Vu** (1910–80), who had been a railway worker in Yunnan, China, before enlisting in the Chinese Nationalist Army when Japan invaded Manchuria, and attending the Huang Pu military school in 1937. When the Kuomintang purged Communist sympathizers, he fled back to Vietnam in 1940, and was imprisoned by the French in 1941–42. He led the Viet Minh troops in Hanoi in late 1946, and (unusually) was appointed simultaneously commander and chief political commissar of the VPA's first formed division, 308th Div, in August 1949.

Le Trong Tan (1914–86) only enlisted in the VPA in 1945, but rose to command 209th Regional Regt in 1950. After a distinctly shaky baptism of fire, this unit redeemed itself later in the Frontier Campaign, and Le Trong Tan soon received command of the newly raised 312th Div. His contemporary **Le Quang Ba** (1914–88) was the first Viet Minh officer from an ethnic minority to rise to senior command. A party member since 1935 and a guerrilla in the Cao Bang region from 1941, he was appointed to command 316th Div, which was partly raised from *montagnards*, on its formation in 1951.

While Communist China's logistical aid to the VPA was fundamental to its victory in 1954, the degree of operational guidance provided by the CMAG remains a vexed question: Chinese commentators naturally tend to play up the CMAG's role, and Vietnamese to play it down. The head of the CMAG, **Wei Guoqing** (1913–89), had risen through battalion, regimental, and divisional commands to an army-group staff appointment in 1949. Sent to Vietnam by Liu Shaoqi in April 1950 at the head of the 280-strong CMAG (plus some 400 junior instructors), he remained in post until July 1954, and led perhaps 20 PLA officers present at Giap's forward HQ near Dien Bien Phu.

Giap claims that they argued against his postponement of the assault initially scheduled for 25 January, but their artillery and engineering advice must certainly have played a significant part in his subsequent preparations. A Chinese source claims that CMAG engineers supervised the construction of Giap's artillery emplacements; one VPA prisoner claimed that there was a Chinese soldier with each 37mm AA gun crew; and in the final 24 hours of the battle, Chinese instructors headed the crews of the dozen 102mm MRLs. Otherwise, the Chinese presence seems to have been limited by this date to Giap's HQ. (While several Foreign Legion prisoners later reported being interrogated by Soviet and East German officers, these were presumably members of observer missions rather than advisers.)

OPPOSING FORCES

FRENCH

Recruitment and organization

By law, no French conscripts could be deployed to Indochina unless they individually volunteered; the CEFEO was a volunteer force, drawn from three distinct organizations. All three were represented at Dien Bien Phu.

A minority of units – by 1953 mostly armour, artillery, engineer, and other specialist support – were created with individual French volunteers, including men from the ranks of the conscript Metropolitan Army which provided France's NATO contingent in Germany. Secondly, the Colonial Troops, descended from the 19th-century Naval Troops, provided a far larger proportion of the CEFEO: mostly French, or French-led Indochinese and West African volunteer units with strong white cadres including some specialist rankers. Finally, the Army of Africa (historically, XIX Army Corps) provided many units of the French Foreign Legion, and French-led Berber and Arab units from Algeria, Morocco, and Tunisia, again with large white cadres.

A further complication was that, since 1951 at the latest, many CEFEO units (though not North or West African battalions) had recruited heavily in Indochina, and by 1953 such battalions had some 50 per cent local rank and file, sometimes fully integrated but more often in separate companies. In 1953–54, of the CEFEO's approximate total of 172,000 regular ground troops, some 52,000 were French (including virtually all the officers); 30,000 were North African; 20,000 were Foreign Legion; 18,000 were West African; and no fewer than 53,000 were Indochinese. (The latter figure does not include either a comparable number of local *supplétif* 'auxiliaries' in semi-regular companies, nor the theoretically 150,000-strong ANV.) Perhaps as many as three-quarters of the CEFEO were tied down in 'sector' commands; in 1953 the only real manoeuvre forces in Tonkin were seven motorized Mobile Groups (GMs – brigades with three infantry battalions plus integral artillery, armour, and services), and eight airborne battalions.

Unit structure and weapons

While the slightly larger airborne battalions were autonomous, and the slightly smaller infantry battalions often formed parts of 3,000-strong administrative regiments, the battalions deployed to Dien Bien Phu had many common features. Units from Europe and Africa were deployed to

Légionnaire of 3 REI posing in winter parade dress. This soldier seems to be in his late 20s; despite popular myth, by 1953 most Wehrmacht veterans had long served their five-year contracts and departed. The Legion in Indochina was still perhaps half German, but only a hard core of re-enlisted NCOs had World War II experience (which proved valuable at Dien Bien Phu). By 1953/54 the Vietnamese companies attached to Legion infantry units in 1951 had been split off to form battalions of the ANV, as always intended. (Carl Mydans/The LIFE Picture Collection/Getty Images)

Indochina more or less for the duration, theoretically kept up to strength with individual replacements. In fact, when in the field, they were usually well below establishment strength; this was due not only to slow replacement of casualties and of personnel repatriated at the end of their tours, but also to the need to leave a sizeable depot element out of battle. For instance, 1 BPC had a total strength of 911, of whom 413 were Vietnamese, but for *Castor* on 20 November 1953 it jumped with only 722. The 6 BPC jumped 651 strong, and II/1 RCP with only 569. Again, while the infantry battalion establishment was 820, on 13 March 1954 the ration strength of the Legion's III/13 DBLE was only 517.

For years, battalions had also been chronically short of officers (sometimes as few as 11, instead of 18), and of senior NCOs (about 40, instead of at least 60). The average age of CEFEO enlisted men (i.e. ranks up to corporal-chief) was at least 28, and some officers were over-age for their ranks – in 1953 lieutenants averaged nearly 33, and captains 38. A proportion of officers were also 'converts' from branches other than the infantry, who arrived only partially trained in their new role.

A battalion was structured as a strong HQ and Services Company (*Compagnie de Commandement et des Services* – CCB) and four numbered rifle companies. The CCB had admin, logistic, signals, transport, intelligence, and medical sections; it also included a mortar platoon (4 x 81mm) and a pioneer platoon (including 4 x 57mm recoilless rifles). When in static defence, a CCB might also receive a few .50-cal. heavy machine guns and flame-throwers.

The rifle company, of anything between 90 and 120 men, officially had three officers, but often only two; a command section, with a radio; a support platoon (2 x rifle-calibre machine guns, 2 x 60mm mortars); and either three or four rifle platoons (in French, *sections*), often led by senior NCOs for lack of officers, and dependent on field telephones for communications.

The basic platoon had three squads (in French, *groupes*). At full strength the ten-man squad had a sergeant commander and two corporal team leaders armed with SMGs; a three-man light machine-gun team with an LMG and two rifles; two other riflemen, a marksman, and a rifle-grenadier. The choice for a company to form four platoons each of two squads, instead of three platoons each with three squads, increased tactical flexibility for fire and movement. The whole platoon could then re-shuffle its assets into one assault squad including all six of the marksmen and rifle-grenadiers, and one fire-support squad with all three LMGs, each squad with plentiful junior leaders.

By 1953 infantry battalion weapons were the French 7.5mm MAS36 bolt-action rifle (plus a minority of the semi-automatic MAS49); the US .30-cal. M1 carbine; the 9mm MAT49 SMG, and 7.5mm FM24/29 LMG; the US .30-cal. M1919 and .50-cal. M2 machine guns, and some old 7.5mm French M31A Reibels; the French M27/31 or US M2 81mm, and French

M35 60mm mortars; the US 57mm M18 recoilless rifle, and the US M1 or M2 flame-thrower.

The combat experience of the specific units deployed to Dien Bien Phu is relevant. The official duration of a soldier's Indochina tour was two years, but in practice it could last as long as 30 months, and many battalion and company commanders and senior NCOs were by now on their second or even third tour since 1946. The exhausting climate and terrain, and the nervous strain, inevitably wore down units and individuals as their tours progressed.

Airborne units

The tempo of operations for airborne battalions, as the CEFEO's only true strategic reserve, was particularly demanding, since they were employed as a 'fire brigade' of elite light infantry.

Combat jumps might alternate between brigade-size offensive operations and single-battalion missions. In few such cases was there any means of extraction except gruelling cross-country foot retreats. When flown into an airstrip, units alternated digging in for defensive fighting with long jungle operations, which were essentially 500-man fighting patrols. Battalions were also deployed on major cordon-and-search operations in the Delta; these might last two months at a time, involving a constant trickle of casualties to mines and booby traps as well as sudden encounter actions.

Any distinction between the Metropolitan, Colonial and Legion para battalions making up Airborne Troops Indochina was by now practically meaningless. A representative example of unit experience is provided by the single nominally Metropolitan battalion, II/1 RCP. This had in fact been raised in Brittany in 1952 as 10 BPC, being retitled on arrival in Vietnam that December for purely traditional reasons (in World War II the Parachute

The 'Bigeard cap', worn with the common US spotted-camo jacket and British 'windproof' camo trousers, identifies this Vietnamese para at Dien Bien Phu shortly after Operation *Castor* as serving with 6 BPC. (For other uniform and equipment details, see the battlescene commentary on page 56). The record of Maj. Bigeard's 6 BPC typified the punishing tempo of operations demanded of para units; *Castor* was their fourth combat jump since arriving in-country in July 1952. Their first, in October 1952, had been a virtually sacrificial mission to Tu Le during the 312th Div's rampage through the Thai Highlands, which cost them heavy casualties. Only two months later they had jumped back into the 'High Region' to spend four months operating out of Na San. After a further month in Laos they got just two weeks' rest, before jumping with 8 BPC and 2 BEP in Operation *Hirondelle* in June 1953, to raid VPA depots around Lang Son; and finally they spent August–October on operations in the Delta, before *Castor* in November. (Corbis via Getty Images)

Light Infantry Regiment, RCP, had been Free France's first airborne unit). Its CO was the 40-year-old Maj. Jean Bréchignac, a World War II paratroop veteran who had commanded companies both in the Vosges and Alsace in 1944–45 and during his first Indochina tour in 1947–49.

In January 1953, shortly after disembarkation, II/1 RCP was flown into the Thai Highlands to carry out repeated deep-penetration missions from Na San. In May it was flown to the Plain of Jars in Laos, carrying out three operations there before flying to Hanoi in mid-June. After ten days' rest and an airborne exercise, in late July it dropped north of Hue, Annam, during the coastal Operation *Camargue*. At the beginning of August it was flown to Seno in Laos, where it constructed defensive positions and carried out probing missions before returning to Hanoi on 20 October (its previously segregated rifle companies now being integrated 50/50 European/ Vietnamese). From 24 October to 6 November it fought around Doi Chua and Lai Cac during Operation *Mouette*, and it had only returned to Hanoi a couple of weeks before jumping with GAP 1 in Operation *Castor*.

Several para units had an even higher work rate during several years of continuous service in Indochina; for instance, by September 1953 the Legion's 1 BEP (in whole or in part) had already made seven jumps. It should also be noted that after II/1 RCP, 1 and 6 BPC were withdrawn from Dien Bien Phu in mid-December 1953, they were all committed to demanding operations in Laos in January–February 1954, before jumping back into Dien Bien Phu for the second time in March and April.

The lack of the red beret was the only obvious difference of the two Foreign Legion para battalions, which had both arrived in winter 1948/49. The 1 BEP had the melancholy distinction of having been completely re-formed after being wiped out during the 'disaster of RC4' in October 1950. Both BEPs had then helped defeat Giap's Dong Trieu offensive in March–April 1951, and had been subject to the usual relentless pace of operations ever since. Both had fought in the RC6/Hoa Binh battles of winter 1951/52; had made combat jumps during Operation *Lorraine* north-west of the Delta in October 1952; and had defended Na San in December 1952. For *Castor*, 1 BEP jumped 653 strong, of whom 336 were Vietnamese (despite the fact that the BEPs' orders of battle list only one nominally Indochinese company – CIPLE – for each). The strong Foreign Para Heavy Mortar Company (1 CEPML) had been formed from the two BEPs.

A unique unit at Dien Bien Phu was Capt. Botella's 5 BPVN, created only in September 1953, but around men who had already served in the two Indochinese companies of the battle-hardened 3 BPC. André Botella, a 'blackfoot' from Algeria, had distinguished himself in 1944 with the Free French 4th SAS. Before *Castor* the 5 BPVN had fought in the major Operation *Brochet* in the Delta in October. The establishment of a Vietnamese para battalion ('*bawouan*') was about 12 French and 22 Indochinese officers; 58 and 51 senior NCOs; and 67 and 616 enlisted men. This unit has been unjustly denigrated by some commentators, but it was among those central to the defence of Dien Bien Phu right up to the final hours.

Infantry

The four battalions of Legion infantry at Dien Bien Phu had all been in-country since 1946, taking part in the pacification of Cochinchina and Annam before transferring up to Tonkin. Infantry companies there had initially been scattered in small posts for local and road security, which made them vulnerable and wasted their potential. Strung-out on trails in the jungle hills, III/3 REI (like 1 BEP) had been annihilated in October 1950.

Beginning with the defeat of Giap's Delta offensives in January–June 1951, entire Legion and North African battalions had then been rotated through motorized *Groupes Mobiles* alongside armour and artillery, greatly improving their cohesion and effectiveness. They had alternated cordon-and-search and reaction missions against VPA 'regionals' in the Delta with offensive operations against the main force. Three of the units at Dien Bien Phu had fought in the RC6/Hoa Binh battles in winter 1951/52, and the exception – the re-formed III/3 REI – at Na San. In addition, the two Legion Composite Heavy Mortar companies (1 and 2 CMMLE), raised from 3 and 5 REI respectively, were recent descendants of a single company that had fought at Na San.

The four North African *tirailleur* battalions were recruited from tough Berber highlanders in Algeria and Morocco. The II/1 RTA had been in-country since September 1949, and were veterans of both Vinh Yen and the Day River in 1951, of RC6/Hoa Binh in winter 1951/52, and of Na San a year later. The III/3 RTA had been shifted all round Indochina since arriving in December 1949: to That Khe in the Chinese border country (though luckily not in autumn 1950); then to restless Thu Dau Mot province in Cochinchina, to Cambodia, to Annam, and finally back to Tonkin. Another unit from the hills of Constantine province was V/7 RTA; since disembarking in May 1951 it had spent its entire service in the Delta. So too had I/4 RTM, which had arrived at the end of 1950 during the crisis following the RC4 disaster. These Moroccans had earned respect fighting on RC6, and in Operation *Lorraine*, Gen. Salan's combined-arms thrust into the Viet Minh rear around Phu Doan in October 1952. They had then fought in the Delta, winning a unit citation.

The Thai troops present at Dien Bien Phu, both in regular battalions (BT 2 and 3) and in separate auxiliary companies, are often unjustly dismissed; some did indeed desert, but others fought bravely to the end. The battalions had been raised as early as 1947 and 1949, and BT 3 had earned an army citation in 1951; but their performance since then had undeniably been mixed, and the enemy's occupation of their home regions in late 1952 had badly damaged their morale. The auxiliary companies had received only brief training and light equipment; brave and skilful jungle fighters, they were quite unsuited for holding trenches under shellfire.

A young North African *tirailleur* ('*turco*'). The Algerian and Moroccan units were mostly recruited from Berber highlanders, and at Dien Bien Phu many fought more stubbornly than racist myth would later claim. However, all four battalions suffered from the usual shortage of experienced French company officers. All the non-European units, being drawn from tribal cultures, particularly depended upon personal leadership, and when trusted officers fell their men sometimes gave way under attack. (Howard Sochurek/The LIFE Picture Collection/ Getty Images)

Other arms

The composite tank squadron of 1st Light Horse Regt (1 RCC) included one platoon ('Blue') from the confusingly named *Régiment d'Infanterie Coloniale du Maroc* (RICM), a mechanized regiment incorporating both armour and

The West African gunners of II/4 RAC proved admirably solid under relentless fire, despite their vulnerability in their open 'all-azimuth' gunpits. During VPA assaults the artillery's expenditure of ammunition was enormous, and simply serving the guns for hours on end was exhausting work. Keeping them serviceable was also a constant task, since the recoil cylinders were often punctured by shell fragments. Despite the almost complete failure of its counter-battery fire, the artillery was absolutely central to the survival of GONO for 55 nights. This soldier, with ritual tribal face scars, wears the red-piped black *calot* cap and gold anchor badge of the Colonial artillery. (Howard Sochurek/The LIFE Picture Collection/Getty Images)

infantry. In the two RCC platoons the crews were half-and-half Europeans and Vietnamese, while the RICM platoon was all-European. The past experience of M24 Chaffee crews had been largely in *Groupements Blindés*, armoured battalion groups in which they were accustomed to operating in close support of integral infantry.

One of the two Colonial artillery battalions (*groupes*) with 105mm howitzers (III/10 RAC), and the single battery of 155s (11/IV/10 RAC), were manned by Moroccans with French cadres; the second 105mm battalion (II/4 RAC) was West African. Since 1951, 105mm battalions in Tonkin had been assigned to the Mobile Groups (e.g. III/10 RAC had been organic to GM 9). Both battalions were well accustomed to providing accurate infantry-support shoots, though at Dien Bien Phu they were hampered by lack of adequate maps.

Air Force
The Air Force in Tonkin (GATAC/Nord) had two squadrons of B-26 (A-26 Invader) twin-engined bombers based in the Delta, totalling 34 aircraft; however, crew shortages reduced the average number available for missions on any given day by about one-third. Fighter-bomber strength was two Air Force squadrons theoretically totalling 32 F8F Bearcats (but again, with fewer pilots) mostly based at Hanoi, plus a third unit of about 12 Navy F6F Hellcats from the carrier *Arromanches*. The Navy also contributed a dozen SB2C Helldiver dive-bombers, and, based at Haiphong, five PB4Y-2 Privateer four-engined heavy bombers (a modification of the B-24 Liberator).

During the battle none of these could be committed solely to missions over Dien Bien Phu, since a proportion had to be flown against the VPA supply routes, and others against targets elsewhere. For example, during the month of April 1954, at the height of the battle, the B-26s flew a total of 423 individual missions over Dien Bien Phu – a total later judged by the B-26 veteran Gen. Champenoux de la Boulaye to be a fraction of what was theoretically possible. In the same month the Navy's couple of dozen Hellcats and Helldivers together flew a more impressive 569 missions, and the handful of Privateers a truly remarkable 176. All ground-attack missions were handicapped by inadequate briefings and target identification, and the lack of real-time radio forward air control from the ground.

The Air Force's transport group (S/GMMTA) was also weakened by shortages of aircrew in particular, and by conflicting demands from several ground operations. The training of C-47 Dakota crews could not keep up with America's supply of aircraft. The three Dakota squadrons then in the Delta managed to put 65 C-47s into the air for Operation *Castor*, but by one point in April 1954 only 55 fit crews were available for the theoretical strength of 101 Dakotas in four squadrons. The couple of dozen C-119 Packets were also limited by an even more drastic shortage of trained French crews, which was only partly made up by American civilians under CIA contract.

There were only 30–40 helicopters in the whole of Indochina. While occasionally making recce or liaison flights, these were normally limited to casualty evacuation – in which role they played only a minimal part at Dien Bien Phu.

VIETNAM PEOPLE'S ARMY

The divisions committed to the assaults on Dien Bien Phu and operating in their immediate rear totalled about 58,800 regular VPA troops. The infantry formations had no motor vehicles, few integral heavy weapons or radios, sparse medical facilities (and, of course, no armoured or air support). The 304th, 308th, 312th, and 316th divisions were each roughly 10,000 strong, though the first of these was only partially present; they were supported by one independent infantry regiment, and the artillery and engineers of 351st Div.

Each infantry division had three infantry regiments, each of three battalions. Each 635-strong battalion comprised an HQ company, and one heavy-weapons and three rifle companies. The HQ company had command and political sections, and comms-and-liaison (including runners), recce-and-intelligence, and engineer platoons. The heavy-weapons company had four medium machine guns, two 81/82mm mortars, and two 60mm or 90mm 'bazookas'.

VPA infantry resting in a shallow assembly trench. They wear light equipment, with little more than an all-purpose haversack, a canteen, and a 'horseshoe roll' containing a sleeping-mat; here their weapons are mixed French captures and Chinese Type 50 'burp guns'. Obviously, the rattan helmets gave no protection except from the weather. By March 1954 most of the units present at Dien Bien Phu had been seasoned by at least three years of hard campaigning in North Vietnam and Laos, but April would see the ranks of partly destroyed battalions filled out with green replacements. (SeM Studio/ Fototeca/Universal Images via Getty Images)

Within the boundaries of the Dien Bien Phu Front alone, 230 miles of roads and tracks had to be repaired, improved, or built from scratch to allow the movement of trucks to the forward depots and artillery and AA guns around the perimeter; VPA engineers routinely had to be assisted by infantrymen, as well as *dan cong* (civilian) labourers. During the 'strangulation' phase in April, assault troops would also spend long nights digging trenches and saps ever closer to the French positions, in danger from mortar and artillery fire and trench raids. (Collection Jean-Claude Labbe/Gamma-Rapho via Getty Images)

(There seems to be little direct evidence for the types of MMGs available apart from French/US captures, but previously the VPA had employed Japanese, French Hotchkiss, and British Vickers guns.) The rifle company had a squad with two 60mm mortars, and three rifle platoons each with a two-gun LMG squad and three assault squads. (For additional divisional and regimental elements, see *Orders of Battle/VPA*).

The infantry's organic heavy-weapons elements have been exaggerated in previous accounts (including the present author's *The Last Valley*). Recent research by Boylan and Olivier suggests that a division had only an organic AA machine-gun battalion and possibly one company of 'DKZ' 57mm RCLs (captured US M18 or Chinese Type 36). Each regiment had one company of six 81/82mm mortars, and another with four to six 57mm RCLs. It seems that some older, locally made 'SKZ' smoothbore recoilless weapons, and some firing over-calibre spigot projectiles, were also present, but their distribution is unknown. In particular, there is no evidence that any of the oft-mentioned 75mm RCLs (captured US M20 or Chinese Type 51) were present before 24 April (see *Orders of Battle/VPA*). (For a note on VPA small arms, see the battlescene commentary on page 76.)

In 1950–51 the *Chu Luc*'s first divisions had been created by 'regularizing' 25,000 men of 'regional' units around an armature of veteran regulars, and rotating them through camps inside China for equipment and training. By 1954 those who survived had long experience of battles all over northern Indochina, and – due to the frontal-assault tactics in which they were trained by the Chinese, and their previously weak artillery support – they had often suffered heavy casualties. In practice, the Communist system of joint command by line officers and political commissars down to company level does not seem to have been as negative as we might expect. It is certainly true that unit command and control was badly handicapped by a doctrine that emphasized rigid obedience to the briefed plan rather than battlefield initiative by battalion and company officers, but a proportion of them had inevitably learned from experience to be more versatile.

The records of some of the regiments present can be traced back to the autumn 1950 Frontier Campaign. All four divisions had been brutally blooded in the failed Delta offensives of early 1951; the 304th, 308th, and 312th Divs had fought the RC6/Hoa Binh battles the following winter; the 308th, 312th, and 316th had penetrated the Thai Highlands in late 1952, culminating in the battle of Na San; and in February–April 1953 the same divisions had advanced deep into Laos (although seeing little combat there).

The conscript *bo doi* in the ranks were unpaid, usually illiterate, and often homesick for their villages down on the plains. In the hostile highland environment, their equipment was basic; on campaign, delivery of their rations was often unreliable; disease was frequent, and medical care

rudimentary. But the hardships of long campaigns had seasoned them; their patriotism and confidence in their commanders were high, and many were highly motivated and courageous.

However, they were closely monitored by unit commissars and the Party members spread throughout the ranks, and from their reports it is clear that morale in the units sacrificed during the 'Battle of the Five Hills' suffered badly. It was naturally even lower among the young and sketchily trained replacements pressed into the ranks thereafter.

Since they proved crucial to the VPA's victory, the amount of field and AA artillery available to the siege army is a long-argued subject, but now seems to be confirmed (see *Orders of Battle*). The 45th Arty Regt of 351st Div had just 24 captured US 105mm howitzers, served by crews with only basic skills. These were backed up by 675th Arty Regt with mixed equipment: 18–20 75mm pieces (mainly old Japanese mountain guns, with a few US M1 pack howitzers), and 16–20 120mm heavy mortars. Despite its title, 237th Arty Regt had either 36 or 54 81/82mm mortars. In all these calibres, the siege army began the battle with significantly less stockpiled ammunition than GONO (a shortage that would recur following the various assault phases, when shoots had to be rigorously rationed until resupply arrived by road).

As for 367th AA Regt, whose threat had such an effect on French resupply and reinforcement, around the valley itself Gen. Giap deployed two AA battalions (383rd and 394th), each with mixed equipment of 12 37mm Russian M1939 automatic cannon (comparable to the 40mm Bofors gun) plus 12 12.7mm heavy machine guns. The organic AA units of the infantry divisions brought the number of AA MGs in and around the valley up to about 85 by mid-March 1954.

It is usually stated that the 24 US 105mm M2 howitzers used by 45th Arty Regt were captured by the Chinese PLA in Korea in 1950–51, but it seems that four had in fact been captured by the VPA from the French, and some of the PLA-supplied guns may have been more elderly ex-Nationalist Chinese weapons acquired in 1949. At Dien Bien Phu each battery was trained for direct fire on specific targets located by scout teams before 13 March. This proved effective; but their dug-in emplacements, with little space for traversing, apparently prevented crews from switching targets to concentrate fire to meet later French counter-attacks. The relocation of four of the six batteries before the second assault phase at the end of March must have negated the original fire plans, making further demands on the crews' limited skills. (Collection Jean-Claude Labbe/Gamma-Rapho via Getty Images)

ORDERS OF BATTLE

French

This lists units known to have been entirely or partially present at Dien Bien Phu *at any date between 13 March and 7 May 1954*, with dates of arrival if after 13 March. Between 20 November 1953 and 13 March 1954 there had been several French unit withdrawals and replacements – notably, the rejection of most of the infantry from Lai Chau originally intended for the garrison, and the withdrawal for operations elsewhere of four of the six para battalions dropped in during Operation *Castor*.

Only combat, combat support, and medical units are fully identified below. Companies within battalions are not identified individually. Infantry battalions had four numbered rifle companies (1st–4th in airborne battalions and in the first battalion of each multi-battalion regiment, 5th–8th in the second battalion, and 9th–12th in the third battalion – although at one time 1 and 2 BEPs numbered their companies in a single sequence, 1st–8th). The same applied to batteries in artillery battalions (*groupes*). The original French airborne and mobile brigades (GAPs and GMs) in/from which some units arrived at Dien Bien Phu are identified, but by the time the battle began on 13 March these identities were redundant.

'Foreign' in a unit title indicates Foreign Legion. Words in parentheses refer to abbreviated designations; successive commanding officers, in original ranks; and initial equipment, where relevant.

OPERATIONAL GROUP NORTH-WEST (GONO; COL. DE CASTRIES)

AIRBORNE INFANTRY

1st Airborne Group (GAP 1; in Nov 1953, Lt.-Col. Fourcade)
6th Colonial Parachute Battalion from 16 March (6 BPC; Maj. Bigeard, Capt. Thomas)
2nd Bn/1st Para Light Inf Regt from 1–6 April (II/1 RCP; Maj. Bréchignac)
(part) 1st Colonial Para Bn from 3–6 May (1 BPC; capts de Bazin de Bezon, Pouget)
2nd Airborne Group (GAP 2; Lt.-Col. Langlais)
1st Foreign Para Bn (1 BEP; Maj. Guiraud)
8th Para Shock Bn (8 BPC; Capt. Tourret)
5th Vietnamese Para Bn from 14 March (5 BPVN; Capt. Botella)
2nd Foreign Para Bn from 10–12 April (2 BEP; Maj. Liesenfelt)
Composite Foreign Para Bn created *in situ* 24 April (BMEP; Maj. Guiraud)

INFANTRY

Mobile Group 6 (GM 6; Lt.-Col. Lalande)
2nd Bn/1st Algerian Rifles Regt (II/1 RTA; Capt. Jeancenelle)
5th Bn/7th Algerian Rifles Regt (V/7 RTA; majs de Mequenem and Kah)
3rd Bn/3rd Foreign Infantry Regt (III/3 REI; Maj. Grand d'Esnon)
Mobile Group 9 (GM 9; Lt.-cols Gaucher, Lemeunier)
1st Bn/13th Foreign Legion Half-Brigade (I/13 DBLE; Maj. Coutant)
3rd Bn/13th Foreign Legion Half-Brigade (III/13 DBLE; Maj. Pégot)
3rd Bn/3rd Algerian Rifles Regt (III/3 RTA; Capt. Garandeau)
(ex-GM 4) 1st Bn/2nd Foreign Infantry Regiment (I/2 REI; Maj. Clémencon)
(ex-GM 7) 1st Bn/4th Moroccan Rifles Regt (I/4 RTM; Maj. Nicolas)
(ex-Lai Chau) 2nd Thai Bn (BT 2; Maj. Chenel)
(ex-GM Vietnamien) 3rd Thai Bn (BT 3; Maj. Thimonnier)
Thai Military Auxiliary Cos (CSMs) and Thai Light Aux Cos (CSLTs)
Companies numbered 272, 413–418, 431–434 and 454.
CSM/CSLT distinction is contradictory in sources, and meaningless in practice.

ARTILLERY (COL. PIROTH, LT.-COL. VAILLANT)

2nd Bn (West African)/4th Colonial Arty Regt (II/4 RAC; Maj. Knecht; 105mm x 12)
3rd Bn (Moroccan)/10th Colonial Arty Regt (III/10 RAC; Maj. Alliou; 105mm x 12)
11th Bty (Moroccan), 4th Bn/4th Colonial Arty Regt (11/IV/4 RAC; Capt. Déal; 155mm x 4)
(section) 35th Para Lt Arty Regt from 6? April (35 RALP; 75mm RCL x 4?)

HEAVY MORTARS AND HMGS

1st Foreign Para Hvy Mortar Co (1 CEPML; Lts Molinier, Turcy, Bergot; 120mm x 12)
1st Foreign Composite Hvy Mortar Co (1 CMMLE; Lts Colcy, Poirier; 120mm x 8)
2nd Foreign Composite Hvy Mortar Co (2 CMMLE; Lt. Fetter; 120mm x 8)
(section) 1st Colonial Far East AA Bn (1 GAACEO; Lt. Redon; .50-cal. quadmounts x 4)

ARMOUR

3rd Composite Sqn/1st Light Horse Regt (3 EM/1 RCC; Capt. Hervouët; M24 Chaffee x 10)
(in Claudine) Command tank 'Conti'; Blue Platoon 'Bazeille', 'Douaumont', 'Mulhouse'; Red Platoon 'Ettlingen', 'Posen', 'Smolensk'
(at Isabelle) Green Platoon 'Auerstaedt', 'Ratisbonne', 'Neumach'

ENGINEERS

(part) 31st (Moroccan) Engineer Bn (31 BG; Maj. Sudrat)

MEDICAL

29th Mobile Surgical Team (29 ACM; Dr Grauwin)
44th Mobile Surgical Team (44 ACM; Dr Gindrey)
3rd Parachute Surgical Team from 16 March (3 ACP; Dr Rézillot);
6th Para Surg Team from 17 March (6 ACP; Dr Vidal); 5th Para Surg Team from 12 April (5 ACP; Dr Hantz)

OTHER SERVICE UNITS

Signals cos x 3
Repair cos (parts) x 3
Provost Bn (part)
Command and Services cos x 3
Intendance (QM) Bn
Munitions Resupply Co
Fuel Resupply Co
Transport Co
Traffic Control Company

AIR FORCE (MAJ. GUÉRIN)

Base Detachment 195 (DB 195); Signals cos 21/374 and 814 (CTA 374 and 814)
(part) Fighter Group 1/22 'Saintonge' (GC 1/22; Capt. Payen; F8F Bearcat x 6–17)
(part) Artillery Air Observation Group 21 (GAOA 21; Lt. Asselineau; MS 500 Criquet x 6–8)
(part) Light Med Evac Co 1 (CLES 1: WO Dufeu? Sikorski H-19 x 1)

Vietnam People's Army

The VPA orbat is taken from Boylan and Olivier (see *Further Reading*), as the best currently available; however, its compilers point out that it cannot be absolutely final – for one thing, VPA units were often assigned duplicate designations for reasons of deception.

Because VPA battalion companies were individually numbered, they are identified below. Heavy weapons companies within infantry battalions are identified where known, but some remain unidentified. In many cases the function of sub-units under direct divisional and regimental command remains unknown (indicated by '?'). Divisional and regimental units are listed here in functional rather than numerical sequence, where known, with unidentified companies listed last.

304TH INFANTRY DIVISION 'NAM DINH' (-)
(CO: HOANG MINH THAO)

Divisional troops (? = identity uncertain; * = presence at Dien Bien Phu uncertain):
20th Intel-Recce Co*
77th Guard Co*
128th Eng Co*
161st Comms/Liaison Co*
620th Transport Co*
505th Replacement Bn*
41st ?* and 650th ?* cos
840th Arty Bn (75mm x 6) (final weeks only?)
9th Inf Regt 'Ninh Binh' (entire regt present only in final days)
Regimental troops: 10th Intel-Recce Co; 157th Guard Co; 94th Inf Gun Co (57mm DKZ x 4–6); 126th Eng Co; 162nd Comms/Liaison; 90th ? and 93rd ? cos
353rd Inf Bn (11th, 12th, and 87th Rifle cos, 50th Hvy Wpns Co)
375th Inf Bn (71st, 73rd, and 138th Rifle cos, 75th Hvy Wpns Co)
400th Inf Bn (83rd, 84th, and 86th Rifle cos, 56th Hvy Wpns Co)
57th Inf Regt 'Nho Quan'
Regimental troops: 30th Intel-Recce Co; 158th Guard Co; 55th DKZ Co (57mm x 4–6); 127th Eng Co; 164th Comms/Liaison Co
265th Inf Bn (17th, 18th, 19th, and 98th cos)
346th Inf Bn (50th, 52nd, and 53rd Rifle cos, 51st Hvy Wpns Co)
418th Inf Bn (54th, 59th, and 60th Rifle cos, 61st Hvy Wpns Co)

308TH INFANTRY DIVISION 'VIET BAC'
(CO: VUONG THUA VU)

Divisional troops (? = identity uncertain):
168th Intel-Recce Co
172nd Guard Co
? DKZ Co (57mm)
309th Eng Co
127th Comms/Liaison Co
317th Transport Co
195th ? Co
387th AA Bn (74th, 78th, 241st, 322nd cos; 12.7mm x 18 ?)
36th Inf Regt 'Sa Pa'
Regimental troops:14th Support Co (81/82mm mortar x 6); 16 DKZ Co (57mm x 4–6); 11th Comms/ Liaison Co; 12th Transport Co; 15th ? and 25th ? cos
80th Inf Bn (61st, 62nd, 63rd, and 64th cos)
84th Inf Bn (41st, 42nd, and 43rd Rifle cos, 44th Hvy Wpns Co)
89th Inf Bn (395th, 397th, 399th, and 401st cos)

88th Inf Regt 'Tam Dao'
Regimental troops: 201st Intel-Recce Co; 238th Support Co (81/82mm mortar x 6); 13th DKZ Co (57mm x 4–6); 203rd Comms/Liaison Co; 205th ?, 207th ? and 240th ? cos
23rd Inf Bn (209th, 211th, and 213th Rifle cos, 215th Hvy Wpns Co)
29th Inf Bn (217th, 219th, and 221st Rifle cos, 223rd Hvy Wpns Co)
322nd Inf Bn (225th, 227th, and 228th Rifle cos, 231st Hvy Wpns Co)
102nd Inf Regt 'Ba Vi'
Regimental troops: 251st Intel-Recce Co; 255th Guard Co; 283rd Support Co (81/82mm mortar x 6); 253rd Comms/Liaison Co; 257th Transport Co; 252nd ? and 285th ? cos
18th Inf Bn (259th, 261st, and 263rd Rifle cos, 265th Hvy Wpns Co)
54th Inf Bn (267th, 269th, and 271st Rifle cos, 273rd Hvy Wpns Co)
79th Inf Bn (275th, 277th, and 279th Rifle cos, 281st Hvy Wpns Co)

312TH INFANTRY DIVISION 'BEN TRE'
(CO: LE TRONG TAN)

Divisional troops (? = identity uncertain):
72nd Intel-Recce Co
248th Guard Co
? DKZ Co (57mm)
240th Eng Co
232nd Replacement Bn
244th ? Co
531st AA Bn (26th, 266th, 267th, and 268th cos; 12.7mm x 18 ?)
141st Inf Regt 'Dam Ha'
Regimental troops: 76th Intel-Recce Co; 261st Guard Co; 260th Inf Gun Co (57mm DKZ x 4–6); 252nd ?, 254th ? and 262nd ? cos
11th Inf Bn (241st, 243rd, and 245th Rifle cos, 247th Hvy Wpns Co)
16th Inf Bn (18th, 19th, 20th, and 21st cos)
428th Inf Bn (39th, 58th, and 77th Rifle cos, 670th Hvy Wpns Co)
165th Inf Regt 'Dong Trieu'
Regimental troops: 407th Intel-Recce Co; 401st DKZ ? Co (57mm x 4–6); 405th Comms/Liaison Co; 409th Transport Co; 168th ? and 509th ? cos
115th Inf Bn (501st, 503rd, and 505th Rifle cos, 914th Hvy Wpns co)
542nd Inf Bn (915th, 918th, 924th, and 942nd cos)
564th Inf Bn (527th, 946th, 950th, and 964th cos)
209th Inf Regt 'Hong Gai'
Regimental troops: 74th Intel-Recce Co; 256th DKZ Co (57mm x 4–6); 202nd Eng Co; 288th Comms/Liaison Co; 300th Transport Co; 294th ? and 303rd ? cos
130th Inf Bn (360th, 363rd and 366th Rifle cos, 280th Hvy Wpns Co)
154th Inf Bn (520th, 525th, and 530th Rifle cos, 270th Hvy Wpns Co)
166th Inf Bn (606th, 612nd, and 618th Rifle cos, 290th Hvy Wpns Co)

316TH INFANTRY DIVISION 'BIEN HOA' (CO: LE QUANG BA)

Divisional troops (? = identity uncertain):
170th Intel-Recce Co
630th Guard Co
? DKZ Co (57mm ?)
150th Eng Co
160th Comms/Liaison Co
180th Transport Co
444th ? Co
536th AA Bn (676th, 677th, 764th, and 765th cos; 12.7mm x 18 ?)
98th Inf Regt 'Ba Don'
Regimental troops: 50th Intel-Recce Co; 15th Guard Co; 56th DKZ Co (57mm x 4–6); 19th Comms/Liaison Co; 58th ? and 76th ? cos
215th Inf Bn (34th, 35th, 36th, and 38th cos)
439th Inf Bn (81st, 82nd, and 83rd Rifle cos, 84th Hvy Wpns Co)
938th Inf Bn (91st, 92nd, 93rd, and 94th cos)
174th Inf Regt 'Soc Trang'
Regimental troops: 153rd Intel-Recce Co; 509th Guard Co; 508th Support Co (81/82mm mortar x 6); 151st Comms/Liaison Co; 567th ? Co
249th Inf Bn (315th, 316th, 317th, and 318th cos)
251st Inf Bn (671st, 672nd, 673rd, and 674th cos)
255th Inf Bn (924th, 825th, 826th, and 653rd cos)
Plus, attached from 176th Inf Regt 'Lang Son'/316th Div (see Rear Area Command below):
888th Inf Bn (811th, 812th, 813th, and 319th cos)

351ST HEAVY DIVISION 'LONG CHAU' (CO: DAO VAN TRUONG)

Divisional troops (? = identity uncertain):
37th AA Co
120th Eng Co
128th Comms/Liaison Co
121st Transport Co
3rd ?, 5th ?, 7th ? and 140th ? cos
45th Arty Regt (105mm x 24)
632nd Howitzer Bn (801st, 802nd and 803rd btys)
954th Howitzer Bn (804th, 805th, and 806th btys)
675th Arty Regt (75mm gun x 18 or 20?; 120mm mortar x 20)
83rd Mortar Bn (112th, 113th, 114th, and 115th btys, plus 116th Bty – captured mortars)
175th Mtn Gun Bn (752nd and 753rd btys, plus from late March 754th Bty)
275th Mtn Gun Bn (756th and 757th btys, plus from late March 755th Bty)
237th Arty Regt
413th Mortar Bn (201st, 202nd, and 203rd cos; 81/82mm x 36 or 54?; dispersed to Inf Divs)
? DKZ Bn (three cos; 75mm x 12; from 24 April only; dispersed, x 4 each to 308th and 312th Divs, x 2 each to 304th and 316th Divs)
(part) 224th Rocket Bn (102mm MRL x 12; in action 6–7 May only)
(parts) 367th AA Regt
(Regt totals 37mm x 36, plus 12.7mm x 48, some detached)
381st AA Bn (811th, 812th, 813th btys (37mm x 12) and 814th Bty (12.7mm x 12) from late April only)
383rd AA Bn (815th, 816th, and 817th btys (37mm), 818th Bty (12.7mm))
394th AA Bn (827th, 829th, and 830th btys (37mm), 828th Bty (12.7mm))
Plus 834th Bty (12.7mm) ex-396th AA Bn from mid-March.
(385th AA Bn until late April, and 392nd and 396th AA Bns were retained in rear areas to defend the Viet Bac and/or lines of communication. 533rd AA Bn detached from 304th Div, and 681st AA Bn (a General Staff asset), each with 18 x 12.7mm, also defended supply routes.)
151st Engineer Regt
106th Eng Bn (52nd, 53rd, and 54th cos)
333rd Eng Bn (226th, 250th, 260th, and 270th cos)
444th Eng Bn (309th, 311th, 313th, and 315th cos)
555th Eng Bn (124th, 130th, and 515th cos)
83rd Special EO Disposal Co

DIEN BIEN PHU FRONT REAR-AREA COMMAND

In addition to some AA units as above:
9th Inf Regt 'Ninh Binh'
Detached from 304th Div (see above) for operations against partisans and any further French parachute landings; rejoined siege army first week May.
(part) 176th Inf Regt 'Lang Son'
Detached from 316th Div (see above) for similar operations. For its third bn, see under 174th Inf Regt (above).
Regimental troops: 300th Intel-Recce Co; 327th DKZ Co (57mm x 4–6); 326th Eng Co; 325th Comms/Liaison Co; 329th Transport Co; 328th ? Co
970th Inf Bn (628th, 632nd, 636th, and 580th cos)
999th Inf Bn (320th, 321st, 323rd, and 324th cos)
148th Sept Inf Regt 'Tay Bac'
Regimental troops: 125th Intel-Recce Co; 226th Sept Co (81/82mm mortar x 6); 523rd Comms/Liaison Co; 519th ? and 565th ? cos
910th Inf Bn (220th, 221st, and 225th Rifle cos, 634th Hvy Wpns Co)
920th Inf Bn (250th, 254th, and 255th Rifle cos, 256th Hvy Wpns Co)
930th Inf Bn (511th, 513th, and 515th Rifle cos, 509th Hvy Wpns Co)
Logistical Command (CO: Dang Kim Giang)
77th Inf Regt; Logistical Sector HQs x 3 (at Son La, Tuan Giao, and Na Tau); Comms/Liaison cos x 2; Main Traffic Control Stations x 18; Road Construction Eng Bns x 4; Medical cos x 7 (total personnel 679); Auto Transport cos x 10, with 446 trucks.
Plus in the area of operations, approx 33,300 *dan cong* civilian labourers.

Propaganda photo of a Vietnamese paratrooper under French training, on the cover of the magazine *Indochine Sud-Est Asiatique*, June–July 1953. Local recruitment for the CEFEO was always necessary due to a shortfall of casualty replacements from France, and reached about 50 per cent in some para battalions. Consequently, about 36 per cent of the defenders of Dien Bien Phu would be Vietnamese: 27 per cent regulars, and 9 per cent 'auxiliaries'. (Private collection via Getty Images)

OPPOSING PLANS

FRENCH

In late 1953 Gen. Navarre's forward planning was focused mainly on Operation *Atlante* in Annam, scheduled for January 1954, and it seems unlikely that for the first 12 days of *Castor* he regarded Dien Bien Phu as a permanent operational asset. We may assume that its occupation was originally contingent, and perhaps not irreversible – any more than Na San's had been. However, as simply one chess move, inviting counter-moves on a crowded board, it seemed to promise some rewards.

After the French victory at Na San, several flown-in para units had ranged quite widely through the High Region, where up to 3,500 French-led *montagnard* guerrillas of the so-called Composite Airborne Commando Group (GCMA) also proved genuinely effective. It was hoped that Dien Bien Phu could fulfil the same parallel defensive and offensive purposes as Na San: as a bastion standing in the way of any attempt to invade

During January–February 1954, elements of 8 BPC and 1 BEP did carry out some familiarization training with the tank squadron; here, during a recce mission to the west during January, Vietnamese paras, probably of 1 BEP's 1 CIPLE, ride a Chaffee camouflaged with the characteristic streaks of brown and yellow mud and/or paint. However, there seems never to have been any full-scale rehearsal for a major counter-attack on one of the outlying strongpoints, such as the operation that would attempt to reinforce CR Gabrielle early on 15 March. (Keystone France/Gamma-Rapho via Getty Images).

Laos, and as a hub for external operations by both French paras and local partisans.

(By the time of the first VPA assault on 13 March 1954 these intentions had already proved over-optimistic. Giap's February 'raid' into Laos by 308th Div and troops from Annam had proved that he could threaten Luang Prabang and the upper Mekong at will; French sorties from Dien Bien Phu had generally been frustrating failures; and a combination of French neglect and VPA retaliation had virtually destroyed the GCMA. Thus, by then Dien Bien Phu's only remaining purpose was to win a defensive victory.)

Navarre decided to accept battle at Dien Bien Phu on 3 December 1953. During the fast-moving flow of events and intelligence reports in December 1953–February 1954, it is difficult to pin down 'who knew what, and who recommended what, when'. Many later claimed to have foreseen the eventual disaster, but most reports actually suggest that CEFEO staff officers were simply covering their backs by putting on record the difficulty of carrying out their particular parts in the initial Operation *Castor*. (Read in retrospect, some of the recorded exchanges both before and during the battle certainly seem to exploit the opportunities afforded by the French language for abstract expressions of deliberate ambiguity.)

In simple terms, on learning during the first week of December that VPA formations (the rest of 316th Div, and 308th Div) were on the move, Navarre decided to reinforce Dien Bien Phu. This 'abscess of fixation' for the enemy would not, however, be simply a passive 'hedgehog': it must remain active, directed by an aggressive cavalry officer. French intelligence sources suggested that Giap would be unable to sustain much more than two divisions in the Thai Highlands, and Navarre continued to order the reinforcement of GONO during December and January for a defensive battle.

However, he was aware by Christmas that enemy stores depots nearby could already support three divisions, and, by early in the New Year, that unprecedented VPA artillery and AA assets were on their way. (Even so,

VPA infantry of 316th Div passing through a *montagnard* village of typical stilted houses during their march into the Thai Highlands to eliminate the French base at Lai Chau – a movement which began several days before Operation *Castor*. (SeM/Universal Images Group via Getty Images)

No fewer than 446 of the VPA's total fleet of 628 2½-ton trucks were devoted to the logistic support of the Dien Bien Phu Front; most were these Soviet Molotovas, but a minority were French–US captures. In total, they carried nearly 1.5 million metric tons of equipment, munitions, and supplies to the siege army. The rudimentary dirt roads were often interdicted by the French Air Force; like the roads themselves (over which treetops were sometimes lashed together to form tunnels), the trucks were camouflaged, and they moved mostly at night. (Collection Jean-Claude Labbe/Gamma-Rapho via Getty Images)

during February, when 308th Div was withdrawn southwards to threaten Laos, his staff had to consider whether Giap might in fact decide to avoid battle at Dien Bien Phu.) Despite evidence to the contrary, he continued to hope that the Air Force could seriously degrade the build-up of Giap's troops and supplies; as the weeks passed he hoped for the best, while privately considering the possibility of the worst.

For his part, Maj.-Gen. Cogny always believed that the reserves would be better employed making strikes out of 'his' Delta to discourage VPA attacks on it (as in Operation *Mouette*). He never believed in the long-term occupation of Dien Bien Phu, though he did admit that the initial operation had 'a sporting chance'. Before the operation he ordered Brig.-Gen. Gilles to limit to a minimum the defensive positions he dug (indicating that Cogny hoped that the occupation would be temporary, soon releasing one or both GAPs back into the general reserve). Immediately following the operation's unexpectedly cheap success, he told journalists that Dien Bien Phu would indeed be 'another Na San'; but on 30 November he implicitly made this impossible by ordering that at any one time half the garrison were to be deployed on offensive operations rather than digging-in. Throughout the battle Cogny was persistently defeatist, telling journalists as early as 28 March that GONO's 'carrots were cooked'.

Both generals seem to have accepted, long before the VPA assaults began, that there was no longer any practical prospect of withdrawing GONO by air. The extraction of the much less-threatened Na San garrison had been a costly and risky venture, achieved only with the support of a strong local guerrilla force which now no longer existed, and by the commitment of airlift capacity which was no longer available. Neither is it easy to believe that a half-hearted plan for an overland link-up and extraction by a weak column from Laos (Operation *Condor*) was ever serious.

During the defence of Dien Bien Phu, both generals were reluctant to authorize the parachuting of reinforcement units unless there was a realistic prospect of their actually turning the tide, rather than merely prolonging the agony. (It has been suggested that in one instance – the requested but refused drop of II/1 RCP on 31 March – such a turning-point might even have been achievable.)

Essentially, the high command's 'plan' during April was to hope that the garrison could hold out until some *deus ex machina* could rescue them – either rapid success in the Geneva peace negotiations, or even a dramatic American intervention. Meanwhile, the terms of the signals exchanged between Navarre and Cogny became unforgivably insulting on the one hand, and quasi-mutinous on the other.

VIETNAMESE

Giap's memoir implies that news of *Castor* immediately persuaded the VPA General Staff to respond decisively in the Thai Highlands, but there was some necessary delay in committing their whole reserves to this front. The intended duration and purpose of Dien Bien Phu's occupation were at first unclear; the initial commitment of paras might possibly have been relatively brief, intended to draw troops away from the Delta and thus allow break-outs like Operation *Mouette* in other sectors. Giap had to keep the 312th and 304th divisions in place for four and six weeks respectively to guard against this possibility; but his central commitment to the Thai Highlands was absolutely confirmed at the latest in late January, by his warning to commanders in Annam that they could expect no *Chu Luc* reserves to assist them against Operation *Atlante*. (In the event, they did not need them; that operation, and particularly the part played by the ANV, was a failure.)

The VPA had two methods for offensive operations. 'Fast Strike, Fast Victory' envisaged a major, all-out assault on an objective while secondary attacks on enemy flanks dispersed and unbalanced defenders; it was risky, but it might bring a quick and relatively cheap victory. 'Steady Attack, Steady Advance' was a 'bite-and-hold' doctrine, to destroy enemy assets successively; it was more certain in outcome, but more expensive in time, lives, and resources.

By the end of November 1953, Giap and the General Staff were agreed on a combination of the two. 'Fast Strike, Fast Victory' would be applied against Lai Chau by 316th Div in late January, followed by about 20 days to rest and reinforce. Dien Bien Phu (which we must remember was held in late November by only six light para battalions with one artillery battery) would then be subjected to 'Steady Attack, Steady Advance' by two divisions over about 45 days, from late February to early April, before the rains began.

In the event, however, Lai Chau was abandoned without a fight on 12 December, and over a matter of days 316th Div destroyed the overland part of this withdrawal at very little cost. That division was complete in the hills east of Dien Bien Phu by about 17 December; by 22 December the artillery of 351st Div was on the move,

In addition to the VPA's trucks, every other possible form of transport was pressed into service, including horse- and buffalo-drawn carts and sledges. About 11,600 river boats also carried bulk cargoes such as rice over long distances, mostly down the Red River from the Chinese border crossing at Lao Cai down to Yen Bai. (SeM/Universal Images Group via Getty Images)

and would complete its crossing of the Black River by 4 January. The 308th Div would arrive north of the valley by the end of December, to spread down its west side; on 24 December, 312th Div was ordered to march for Dien Bien Phu, to arrive north-east of it in mid-January, taking position between 308th Div and 316th Div; and on 5 January, just before Giap began his own journey to the Thai Highlands, he finally ordered 304th Div west, to arrive by 24 January south-east of the valley.

While their actual contribution in tonnage has been exaggerated, the Front Supply Commission did make use of about 22,000 of the famous bicycles converted for pushing, with a bamboo cargo-frame that usually carried between 220 and 450 pounds. (SeM/ Universal Images Group via Getty Images)

During the period from mid-December to mid-January, it is clear that the easy capture of Lai Chau enthused some members of the General Staff, CMAG, and some senior officers sent to the front ahead of Giap, with the idea of bringing the assault on Dien Bien Phu forward. They planned to employ 'Fast Strike, Fast Victory' over three nights and two days from 20 January, with the 316th, 308th, and 312th divisions. When Giap arrived on 13 January this was explained to him by Hoang Van Thai, and the enthusiasm of the staff, subordinate commanders, commissars, and Chinese advisors quickly became clear to him.

The core of Viet Minh doctrine was 'only commit to a major attack if assured of victory'. Giap had immediate misgivings, recognizing that the army was unready to launch the most ambitious assault in its history only a week later. (The VPA had never yet successfully taken an entrenched and air-supported French position held by more than two companies.) Many of the troops who were arriving were exhausted by forced marches, and badly supplied. Only a small part of the artillery had been emplaced, inadequately, with far too little ammunition. The building of supply roads and circulation tracks, and – particularly – the digging of the approach trenches that were central to VPA assault tactics, had hardly started. Moreover, by this date GONO had greatly expanded its northern outworks; had exchanged four of its light para battalions for six infantry units of GMs 6 and 9, with more still flying in; and had received 155mm heavy guns, five more 105mm batteries, a tank squadron, and fighter-bombers.

It is clear that if the 'Fast Strike, Fast Victory' formula had been attempted in late January, it would have resulted in disastrous defeat. However, Giap could not make a unilateral decision, and had to buy time by convening conferences and arguing his case patiently. Delay and difficulty in installing the artillery enabled him to order a postponement until 25 January, but on the 24th intelligence confirmed that the French were aware of this. Another 24-hour postponement was agreed; but at a meeting on the morning of 26 January Giap managed to convince the Front Committee that the risks were simply unacceptable, and that the 'Steady Attack, Steady Advance' policy should be re-adopted. Full preparations for a siege should be undertaken, working towards an assault in mid-March.

VPA troops dragging a 105mm howitzer up a jungle hillside to be emplaced on a forward slope. Building each battery's four casemates, five bunkers, and linking trenches took about 200 men up to 15 days to complete. Each casemate required the digging out of 7,000–10,000 cubic feet of earth, and the assembly of foot-thick timbers cut a mile or two away so as not to reveal felling around the position. Each casemate had at least 9 feet of earth and timber overhead cover, and dummy casemates were also built to draw French fire. The gun was fully enclosed, apart from an embrasure that was covered with moveable sandbags and carefully recamouflaged with unscorched foliage between shoots. This enormous effort was almost entirely successful in frustrating French observation and counter-battery fire. (Collection Jean-Claude Labbe/Gamma-Rapho via Getty Images)

This was Giap's most decisive personal achievement of the whole campaign, but it came at the cost of expanding and prolonging the huge demands on the VPA's logistics.

* * *

There is no space here to do justice to the monumental logistic, organizational, and human effort that kept the VPA siege army in action for nearly five months, about 250 miles from their Viet Bac bases and 400 miles from the main Chinese border crossing for supplies and equipment. The French decision to accept battle was based on the belief that Giap could only sustain two-plus divisions in the Thai Highlands. By mobilizing the entire national resources of the DRV, and by conscripting some 250,000 men and women labourers, the Front Supply Commission far surpassed this achievement.

The fundamental task of these *dan cong*, alongside many VPA troops, was repairing, or building from scratch, some hundreds of miles of roads and tracks to make them practical for motor vehicles and artillery. This involved shifting (without mechanical equipment) masses of soil and rock, and constructing innumerable water crossings. Once built, these routes had to be camouflaged, and then maintained, against air attacks which were intermittent, but repeatedly successful at some choke points. The ultimate failure of GATAC/Nord to seriously delay the movement of troops, equipment, and supplies to the siege army should not distract us from the vast scale of the Vietnamese human effort and the sacrifices it involved.

The total of supplies transported within the boundaries of the Dien Bien Phu Front is recorded at just under 1.7 million metric tons. Contrary to legend, this was achieved mainly (84.5 per cent) by means of the Front's Soviet and captured US trucks, though they were backed up by animal-drawn carts and sledges, some 11,600 river boats, about twice that many of the *folklorique* converted bicycles, and, in the most rugged terrain, by thousands of human labourers. The latter were particularly vital for unloading and reloading cargo between trucks operating in relays over individual sections of road, and also for repairing bomb damage. (As always, interested readers will find much supporting material in Boylan and Olivier.)

THE BATTLE

FIRST ASSAULT PHASE: 13–17 MARCH

By 13 March the garrison had been accustomed for weeks to intermittent ranging and harassing fire from the VPA artillery on heights north, north-east, and east of the valley, which their own 155mm howitzers had proved unable to silence. Counter-battery fire was almost wholly ineffective, due both to the difficulty for aerial observers in spotting the VPA gun positions dug in and camouflaged on the forward slopes of the surrounding hills, and to the very solid overhead cover provided for them. During the 13th, VPA shelling added three to the number of transport aircraft already disabled beside the two airstrips.

Officers had been briefed that the VPA assault was expected from 1700hrs, but when the bombardment was unleashed at about 1720hrs, its weight and accuracy came as a shocking surprise – few men in GONO had any past experience of serious shellfire. Fired on carefully registered targets by five 105mm, two 75mm and one 120mm batteries, shells and bombs fell all over the main camp at a rate of 60 per minute – on the command

Command posts in the headquarters area, betrayed by their many tall radio antennae and telephone poles, had been identified as priority targets by VPA scouting parties. The CPs were solidly dug in, with overhead cover topped by this corrugated 'elephant iron', but on 13 March those of both GM 9 and GAP 2 were penetrated and wrecked. In the background, a main fuel dump blazes out of control; the bombardment also detonated a dump of 120mm mortar ammunition. (Keystone France via Getty Images)

posts, the airfield, fuel and ammo dumps, the gun and mortar pits, on CRs Béatrice, Gabrielle, and Dominique – while other batteries also hit Isabelle. The hospital admitted some 150 wounded during that night. Telephone lines were cut, thus delaying situation reports and orders. While some long-stored VPA shells proved to be duds, the damage was still considerable. At least three howitzers in their open pits were disabled, a CEPML mortar platoon was virtually wiped out, and at about 1930hrs the much-respected Lt.-Col. Gaucher was mortally wounded in his wrecked GM 9/Central Sector HQ. His command of the sector was immediately passed – with a confused remit – to Lt.-Col. Langlais of GAP 2, while some GONO staff officers seem to have been effectively paralyzed with shock. The artillerymen served their exposed guns courageously despite casualties, but with little effect.

BÉATRICE

In the far north-east, CR Béatrice comprised company strongpoints on three closely spaced hillocks rising about 60 feet above the north side of RP41, surrounded by woodland on three sides. From heights both to the north and beyond the road to the south, 312th Div had dug assembly and approach trenches, some reaching close to the wire, and patrols had reconnoitred the defences over several nights. This CR was held by III/13 DBLE, a solid but understrength Legion unit; including attached Thai auxiliaries it had only some 500 men on the position, and only one of its companies had even two officers.

From the north, 428th Bn and (reinforced) 11th Bn/141st Regt, and from the south-east 130th Bn/209th Regt, had moved into their forward trenches since mid-afternoon. The bombardment by 105s, 75s, and heavy mortars began at about 1720hrs, while infantry mortars and RCLs in 312th Div's trenches picked off identified targets. Trenches and bunkers collapsed, and

Paras of 8 BPC photographed in inadequate shelter trenches following the bombardment of 13 March. The unusual title of *8e Battalion Parachutiste de Choc* – 8th Shock Parachute Battalion – had little significance. Raised in February 1951 as the 8th Colonial, it had (uniquely) spent winter 1952/53 training for special operations in separate companies alongside the guerrillas of the Composite Airborne Commando Group, but that plan came to nothing, and the renamed unit returned to the general reserve. Its CO from January 1953 was Capt. Pierre Tourret, formerly Maj. Bigeard's deputy in 6 BPC. (Keystone France/Gamma-Rapho via Getty Images)

casualties quickly mounted. Fatally, the battalion CP and its radios were destroyed, the CO and his deputy were killed, and three company officers became casualties; the chain of command was lost, as was the ability to adjust French supporting artillery fire. Nevertheless, from about 1830hrs this support did delay and weaken the dusk infantry assaults – by 141st Regt on Béatrice 1 in the north-east, then pushing on against Béatrice 4 in the north-west; and by 209th Regt on Béatrice 3 in the south-east, while its 164th Bn blocked RP41 against any reinforcement. Savage close-quarter night-fighting on the position lasted for at least six hours; the VPA battalions (who now encountered flame-throwers for the first time) were often checked, and had to call for supporting fire and reserves, before the last French resistance on Béatrice 2 in the south-west ceased at some time between 0130 and 0230hrs.

About 110 *légionnaires* escaped, to join 80 of their battalion already detached in Claudine and Huguette. For various reasons, including confusion over a cunning VPA offer of a truce to collect wounded, no counter-attack was attempted. This was the first time during the whole war that a good, dug-in battalion had been overrun in a single night, and the impact on GONO's morale was deadening. On the afternoon of 14 March 5 BPVN were parachuted in to replace the lost battalion, and began digging in on Eliane 4.

GABRIELLE

Giap's obvious next target was Gabrielle. Held by the Algerian V/7 RTA, 626 strong and reinforced with a Thai CSM, this was a boat-shaped 180-foot-high hill measuring about 500 by 200 yards. It was the best sited and dug-in of all the CRs, and unique in having almost continuous double perimeter

On a PSP track at Hanoi/ Bach Mai Airfield, 16 March, 'Bigeard's boys' prepare to emplane for 6 BPC's second jump over Dien Bien Phu. The foreground paras wear British 'windproof' camouflage uniforms; these 'sausage-skins' were popular for their cool lightness. Their rig consists of the US T5 dorsal main and chest emergency packs, with the TAP M1950 'lightened haversack' slung in front of the groin. The 'canopy first' design of the T5 gave rapid opening for low-altitude jumps, but consequently it had a fairly brutal opening shock. (Joseph Scherschel/The LIFE Picture Collection/Getty Images)

FRENCH

A. 9/III/13 DBLE (Béatrice 1)
B. 11/III/13 DBLE (Béatrice 3)
C. 10/III/13 DBLE (Béatrice 2)
D. 12th Co and HQ of III/13 DBLE (Béatrice 4)
E. 1/V/7 RTA
F. 2/V/7 RTA
G. 3/V/7 RTA
H. 4/V/7 RTA
I. HQ/V/7 RTA plus part of 2 CMMLE plus CSM 416
J. 3rd and 4th Cos of 1 BEP plus Red and Blue tank ptns
K. 5 BPVN
L. 11/BT 3 (Anne-Marie 1)
M. HQ and 10th Co of BT 3 plus a CSM (Anne-Marie 2)

HILL 536

GABRIELLE

BAN KHE PHAI

ANNE-MARIE

BAN KHEO

PAVIE TRACK

308

EVENTS

Night, 13/14 March

1. During bombardment from *c*. 1720hrs, 154th Bn/209th Regt (minus one company) blocks RP41 to prevent reinforcement from main camp.

2. *c*. 1830hrs, 428th Bn/141st Regt takes heavy losses from French artillery while crossing river to assault Béatrice 1. After breaking in at further cost, unit finally takes strongpoint at *c*. 2230hrs.

3. *c*. 1830hrs, 130th Bn/209th Regt crosses RP41 in ready-dug approach trenches and assaults Béatrice 3. Survivors from 11/III/13 DBLE cross to Béatrice 2 at *c*. 2030hrs.

4. *c*. 1830hrs, 11th Bn/141st Regt (plus a company from 154th Bn) assaults Béatrice 4 and 2; heavy losses from French support fire, and pioneers decimated by MGs; reserve 16th Bn committed at 2130hrs, but assault again checked. Renewed 105mm bombardment; Béatrice 2 falls by *c*. 0230hrs; 11th Bn suffers 50 per cent casualties.

Night, 14/15 March

5. After weak bombardment, from *c*. 2030hrs 564th Bn/165th Regt from NW, and 29th Bn/88th Regt followed by 322nd Bn/88th Regt from NE, begin attacks; after pause from 0230hrs, at 0330hrs heavy bombardment begins. 0400hrs, break-in by 564th Bn sealed off; 88th Regt units only penetrate at 0430hrs. Resistance on north of hill ceases *c*. 0730hrs.

6. By *c*. 0430hrs, 542nd Bn followed by 115th Bn/165th Regt penetrate from SE; by 0715hrs active defence reduced to only 2/V/RTA in SW strongpoint.

Morning, 15 March

7. Counter-attack force starts out at 0515hrs (3rd and 4th Cos from 1 BEP, plus seven tanks), followed slowly from 0545hrs by 5 BPVN.

8. *c*. 0630hrs, reaching defended ford and under fire, 1 BEP and tanks ordered to await 5 BPVN. 0730hrs, still alone, they assault and drive VPA back on trenches at Ban Khe Phai.

9. 4/1 BEP engage and mask village position, while rest push on under 75mm and 120mm fire; two damaged tanks withdraw. Meanwhile, 5 BPVN reaches ford under fire, but only part of it crosses before remainder balk and take cover.

10. 3/1 BEP reach foot of Gabrielle; *c*. 0900hrs, V/7 RTA survivors link with them; with artillery support, whole force withdraws to main camp.

15–17 March

11. Disheartened by loss of Béatrice and Gabrielle, by mortaring, and by intense Viet Minh propaganda, 258 Thais of BT 3 and a CSM (*c*. 30 per cent) desert Anne-Maries 1 and 2 on nights of 15/16 and 16/17 March. Remainder are transferred to Isabelle, and Anne-Maries 1 and 2 are abandoned as indefensible.

FIRST ASSAULT PHASE, 13–17 MARCH 1954

Following bombardments late on the afternoon of 13 March, Giap committed two regiments from 312th Div to night assaults on Béatrice, isolated north-east of the main camp. The understrength Legion battalion holding it was submerged after six hours of costly close-quarter fighting. Despite a delay in moving 75mm guns and 120mm mortars west, the following night a regiment each from 308th and 312th Divs overran most of the strong Algerian unit holding the more solid northern outwork, Gabrielle, and an attempted counter-attack by paratroopers and tanks was botched. The north-western strongpoints Anne-Marie 1 and 2 were then abandoned after desertions by Thai troops. Giap's expenditure of ammunition then obliged him to pause, but these first successes left the north of the camp dangerously exposed. (Note that in this book we do not attempt to illustrate the developing VPA trench systems, nor the communication trenches dug to link French positions.)

HILL 701

NAM YUM RIVER

BÉATRICE

VPA
1. Part of 209th Inf Regt/312th Div
2. Part of 141st Inf Regt/312th Div
3. Part of 141st Inf Regt
4. Co from 88th Inf Regt/308th Div and Co from 165th Inf Regt/312th Div plus 75mm bty nearby
5. Bn, 165th Inf Regt and two Bns from 88th Inf Regt
6. Two Bns from 165th Inf Regt

xx
312

Note: gridlines are shown at intervals of 0.5km (0.31 miles)

16 March: The arrival, on a DZ near Isabelle, of 6 BPC, one of only two reinforcement units to be dropped complete and by daylight (the other being 5 BPVN). The subsequent jumps by II/1 RCP, 2 BEP, and most of 1 BPC were necessarily spread over several nights each, since the 'Banjo' Dakotas had to take turns dropping only parts of their sticks during successive passes over the shrinking camp. They also had to pause while parachute flares were being dropped to assist the defensive night-fighting. (Keystone France/Gamma-Keystone via Getty Images)

trenches; these allowed the defenders to reinforce company sectors, or to seal them off. The battalion had been given additional heavy weapons, and had formed a counter-attack reserve platoon including a flame-thrower squad.

Rain on 14 March hampered Giap's westward movement of mountain guns and 120mm mortars, thus seriously delaying the planned assault that night. While 308th Div's staff would command the attack, its units, still tired from their march back from Laos, were supported by 165th Regt, 312th Div's reserve, which had been left out of the battle for Béatrice. The 564th Bn/165th Regt would deliver an assault from the north-west, seconded by 29th and 322nd Bns/88th Regt of 308th Div from the north-east, and by 165th Regt's 542nd and 115th Bns from the south-east.

Just before nightfall a single 105mm battery opened up, along with the infantry units' mortars and RCLs; infantry probed the defences, and French artillery raked assembly areas north and east of the hill. These preliminaries caused casualties on both sides, but it was not until 0330hrs that the long-awaited VPA 75s and heavy mortars finally got into action from closer range. A first infantry penetration from the north at 0400hrs was sealed off by a counter-attack, but two more battalions broke in at 0430hrs, while 165th Regt's units penetrated the south-east perimeter. Then a shell on the CP killed or disabled V/7 RTA's command staff and smashed the radios; communication between companies was disrupted, and from his HQ in the main camp Lt.-Col. Langlais could only make intermittent contact with one of them.

A counter-attack from the main camp was attempted, but badly mishandled. Langlais anticipated only being able to extricate survivors; at 0515hrs he sent Maj. de Séguin-Pazzis with half of 1 BEP and seven tanks, but at 0545hrs he recognized their inadequacy, and ordered 5 BPVN (from the far side of the camp) to follow them. At 0630hrs the Legion paras and tanks reached a ford some 1,500 yards short of Gabrielle, with trenches about 750 yards further on at Ban Khe Phai held by one VPA company each from 88th and 165th Regts. Overestimating their strength, Séguin-Pazzis waited for 5 BPVN to catch up.

At 0700hrs Langlais confirmed to him that he was only to rescue the survivors from Gabrielle, and this signal was overheard by an officer on the hill. By now, despite artillery and quad-.50-cal. support, only the southern part of Gabrielle was still holding out. Séguin-Pazzis then ordered his paras and tanks forward; the ford was crossed and Ban Khe Phai was passed, though at significant cost. Now yet another signal from Langlais told Séguin-Pazzis to decide for himself whether to extricate survivors or try to retake Gabrielle. He inevitably chose the first option when, under VPA shellfire, only half of the finally arrived 5 BPVN obeyed orders to cross the ford.

With French artillery support, 165 defenders were recovered from Gabrielle at around 0900hrs on 15 March. The VPA casualties overnight are unconfirmed, but certainly included several hundred killed. The failure of the counter-attack was unjustly blamed on 5 BPVN, which would later fight heroically; it was actually due to the demoralized GONO staff, who had thrust too much responsibility onto the unprepared Langlais. GONO was now almost naked from the north. Later that day the artillery commander Col. Piroth, devastated by the failure of his counter-battery efforts, committed suicide, and Lt.-Col. Keller, Col. de Castries' chief of staff, collapsed into a nervous breakdown.

GONO had expended two-thirds of its artillery ammunition, but bad weather hampered air operations until 16 March, which brought air-dropped shells, replacement 105s, casualty replacements, the first of two extra medical teams – and Maj. Bigeard's crack 6 BPC, which lifted morale somewhat. However, an attempt to evacuate casualties in Dakotas painted with red crosses was prevented by shellfire, and VPA AA guns were also now emplaced closer to and in line with the runway, making daylight landings and air-drops (which had to approach from the south) riskier.

The feared next assault – on the now exposed CR Anne-Marie, held by the disheartened and under-officered BT 3, plus a CSM – never happened. Many of those holding the hill positions Anne-Marie 1 and 2, subjected to Viet Minh propaganda broadcasts, deserted over the nights of 15/16 and 16/17 March. After the 17th these strongpoints were abandoned as indefensible; the separated Anne-Maries 3 and 4 were redesignated Huguettes 6 and 7, held respectively by companies of I/2 REI and 5 BPVN. The remnants of BT 3 were shifted down to Isabelle.

THE LULL: 17–30 MARCH

During these two weeks both sides re-ammunitioned, consolidated, and patrolled; the VPA exerted itself digging webs of new trenches and saps, which GONO units periodically raided. Two of Giap's 105mm batteries were relocated north of Anne-Marie, one close to Béatrice, and one east of Isabelle. His army was able to incorporate casualty replacements from his local reserve pool of 6,000–8,000 men, but GONO only got specialist replacements dropped in, such as for gun and tank crews – de Castries was denied another para battalion. New fighting positions were dug for the original two para units: 8 BPC in Épervier south of the gun batteries in Dominique 4, and 1 BEP in Junon replacing Claudine 6, each of them with two of the camp's four quad-.50-cal. mounts. Outpost Dominique 6, on RP41 between Dominiques 1 and 2, was also established by a company from 5 BPVN.

From 18/19 March casevac flights were made only after dark, and the tempo of resupply operations was already putting a strain on the Dakota crews. During the week 24–31 March three C-47s were shot down and

Loading wounded – including an African gunner from II/4 RAC – into a Dakota during its brief turn-around halt at the north end of the runway. Casualties had to shelter in the drainage ditch until the last minute, and loading often took place under fire, causing further casualties amid distressing scenes. Daylight casevac flights were abandoned after 18/19 March, when successful tactics for night flights were devised; these were employed over the next nine nights. (AFP via Getty Images)

Major road-clearing actions, 20–30 March 1954

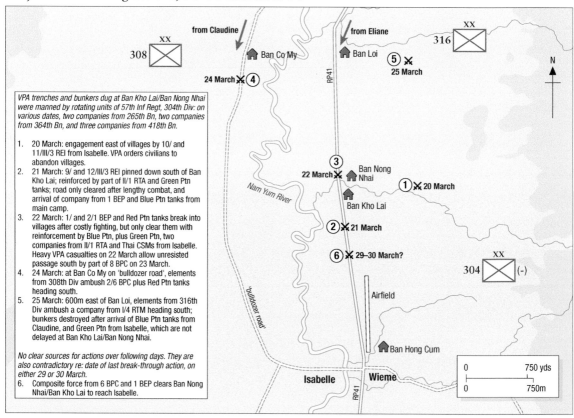

from Claudine

308 XX

Ban Co My

24 March ✗ ④

from Eliane

Ban Loi

⑤ ✗
25 March

316 XX

N

RP41

VPA trenches and bunkers dug at Ban Kho Lai/Ban Nong Nhai were manned by rotating units of 57th Inf Regt, 304th Div: on various dates, two companies from 265th Bn, two companies from 364th Bn, and three companies from 418th Bn.

1. 20 March: engagement east of villages by 10/ and 11/III/3 REI from Isabelle. VPA orders civilians to abandon villages.
2. 21 March: 9/ and 12/III/3 REI pinned down south of Ban Kho Lai; reinforced by part of II/1 RTA and Green Ptn tanks; road only cleared after lengthy combat, and arrival of company from 1 BEP and Blue Ptn tanks from main camp.
3. 22 March: 1/ and 2/1 BEP and Red Ptn tanks break into villages after costly fighting, but only clear them with reinforcement by Blue Ptn, plus Green Ptn, two companies from II/1 RTA and Thai CSMs from Isabelle. Heavy VPA casualties on 22 March allow unresisted passage south by part of 8 BPC on 23 March.
4. 24 March: at Ban Co My on 'bulldozer road', elements from 308th Div ambush 2/6 BPC plus Red Ptn tanks heading south.
5. 25 March: 600m east of Ban Loi, elements from 316th Div ambush a company from I/4 RTM heading south; bunkers destroyed after arrival of Blue Ptn tanks from Claudine, and Green Ptn from Isabelle, which are not delayed at Ban Kho Lai/Ban Nong Nhai.

No clear sources for actions over following days. They are also contradictory re: date of last break-through action, on either 29 or 30 March.

6. Composite force from 6 BPC and 1 BEP clears Ban Nong Nhai/Ban Kho Lai to reach Isabelle.

Nam Yum River

③
22 March ✗   Ban Nong Nhai

Ban Kho Lai

① ✗ 20 March

② ✗ 21 March

⑥ ✗ 29–30 March?

304 XX (-)

Airfield

'bulldozer road'

Ban Hong Cum

0 — 750 yds
0 — 750m

Isabelle   **Wieme**

RP41

one destroyed on the ground, and the transports ceased daylight missions below 6,500 feet; this inevitably caused scattering of parachuted loads. This setback was largely achieved by Giap's heavy AA machine guns; by 19 March

The use of Sikorzski S-55 ('H-19') helicopters to lift loads of four casualties out to Muong Sai in Laos ended after an already-loaded *hélico* was destroyed by enemy fire at Isabelle on 23 March, and a practice night flight on 27/28 March ended in a fatal crash. (ullstein-bild via Getty Images)

This photo was reportedly taken on 19 March, and clearly shows renewed digging-in on one of the hilltop CRs. The barbed wire on the forward slope typically consists of only half a dozen rows of simple 'cattle fencing'. In the aftermath of the VPA's first bombardments anything that might provide better cover was gathered up, particularly ammo boxes to be filled with earth; note the shortage of sandbags in this stretch. Repaired telephone wires were re-laid in grooves along the walls of trenches, though this soldier seems to be digging a niche for ready-use grenades and spare ammo. (Keystone France/Gamma-Rapho via Getty Images)

French bombers had managed to knock out seven of his 37mm AA guns, thus almost silencing the others until the end of the month.

From 24 March the command structure of GONO was rationalized (see *Opposing Commanders*). While patrols clashed around several CRs, the main combats took place during attempts to keep RP41 open down to Isabelle. Penetrating entrenchments dug by 304th Div around Ban Kho Lai and Ban Nong Nhai demanded increasing commitments of troops and tanks from both the main camp and Isabelle. On 30 March these attempts were abandoned; from then on, Isabelle was on its own.

Another major sortie lifted morale. In response to the tightening AA belt, Col. de Castries ordered Maj. Bigeard to plan an attack on 28 March against VPA positions to the west, at the villages of Ban Ban and Ban Ong Pet (see battlescene commentary, page 56). With artillery and some air support, plus the whole tank squadron, 8 BPC and 6 BPC inflicted losses on 308th Div's

Although now dug much deeper, the trenches were so narrow that movements were difficult. Note the earth sacks made of *cai-phen* woven fibre; when wet, these got slippery, and did not pack as well as hessian/burlap sandbags. His Denison smock identifies the foreground para to 8 BPC, and the disabled aircraft in the distance place the photo in the new location Épervier. One is a Morane 500 Criquet spotter (Fieseler Fi 156 Storch), of which none remained operational at Dien Bien Phu after 15 March. The tail in the top right corner seems to be that of a wrecked Curtiss C-46, which became a landmark on the west side of the airstrip just south of strongpoint Huguette 1. (TopFoto)

6 BPC IN ACTION SOUTH-EAST OF BAN ONG PET; C.1500HRS, 28 MARCH 1954 (PP. 54–55)

The so-called 'flak raid' aimed to take out light AA guns of 308th Div, which had been established west of Dien Bien Phu around the villages of Ban Ban and Ban Ong Pet. After artillery and mortar barrages between 0600 and 0650hrs, 8 BPC advanced from 'Claudine' towards Ban Ban supported by the tanks of Blue Ptn, while to the south on their left 6 BPC moved towards Ban Ong Pet, followed by Red Ptn. Both units had to fight their way into and along networks of enemy trenches; resistance was stubborn, by 387th AA Bn and 23rd and 322nd Bns, 88th Inf Regt, and all the para companies were successively committed.

6 BPC knocked out a number of 12.7mm weapons, but were checked by increasing enemy resistance. At midday Green Ptn's tanks were ordered up from Isabelle to support 4/6 BPC on the left flank, where they helped repulse a dangerous counter-attack. In heavy fighting, enemy mortars and AA MGs took an increasing toll, and at about 1500hrs a fighting withdrawal was ordered. This scene, looking roughly north-east, imagines that transition on the left flank, with 4/6 BPC beginning to fall back under covering fire. The day cost the para units 20 killed and 90 wounded, including six officers (e.g. **1**); VPA casualties are unknown, but were probably significant.

* * *

Shortly before Operation *Castor*, para units received new French M1947/51 and /52 camouflage jump uniforms. These are visible in many photos – but so is continuing use of World War II US and British camouflage clothing. The 4th Co (until November 1953, 6 BPC's 23rd Indochinese Para Co – 23e CIPLE) wore white recognition scarves.

At full strength, a ten-man paratroop squad (*groupe de combat*) comprised a sergeant commander (**2**) and two corporal team leaders

(e.g. **3**) armed with SMGs or carbines; a three-man light machine gun team (**4**) with an LMG and two rifles; two *grenadier-voltigeurs* with rifles (e.g. **5**); a marksman (**6**), and a rifle-grenadier (**7**). Here, the Vietnamese fire-team leader (**3**), armed with a 9mm MAT49 sub-machine gun, is throwing a French 'offensive' OF37 concussion grenade, identified by its halved ochre/red paint finish; he wears a US camo jacket. The fibre liner of the US M1 helmet was modified for the paras in-country, with 'reverse A'-straps and chin harness. Airborne Troops (TAP) M1950 web equipment had pairs of double rifle-clip or five-magazine SMG pouches, an M1951 canteen, and often a US M3 fighting knife on the belt and a para first-aid pouch taped to the left suspender. In this action nearly all troops carried the TAP 'lightened haversack'.

Widespread issue of SMGs and carbines made it necessary to provide a *tireur d'élite* (**6**) for each squad, here with a semi-automatic 7.5mm MAS49 rifle fitted with an optical sight. The French sergeant squad leader (**2**) wears a re-tailored British windproof 'sausage-skin' smock. He carries a folding-butt M1A1 carbine; behind him, a trooper (**5**) has the CR39 airborne version of the 7.5mm MAS36 rifle, with a folding aluminium buttstock. At far right, a grenadier (**7**) aims a MAS36 fg48, with muzzle launcher and sight for 50mm rifle grenades.

During this action the M24 tank 'Neumach' (**8**) of Lt. Préaud's Green Ptn, commanded by Sgt. Philip, was damaged but not disabled. The Chaffee displays the type of two-colour paint and mud-smear camouflage applied individually by the crews over the olive-drab factory finish. Photos show the tanks operating with all hatches fastened and no external stowage.

AAMG battalion and 88th Inf Regt before making a controlled withdrawal, at a cost of 110 casualties.

However, on the same day the airfield was finally closed to all movements; from now on men and matériel could only be dropped by parachute. The casualties would steadily accumulate in the underground hospital, which had to be greatly extended.

SECOND ASSAULT PHASE: 30 MARCH–5 APRIL – 'BATTLE OF THE FIVE HILLS'

On 28 March Giap had briefed his commanders for the ambitious second assault phase, planning to eliminate all of GONO's eastern bastions – the two hilltops of Dominique and the three of Eliane – in a single night. With preparatory and support fire from 351st Div, units of 312th Div were to capture Dominiques 1 and 2. A unit detached (oddly) from 308th Div on the western front was to eliminate outpost Dominique 5 and press on to Dominique 3 near the riverbank. Units of 316th Div were assigned Elianes 1, 4, and 2. Meanwhile, in the west, 308th Div was to feint against Huguette and Claudine, to block the 'bulldozer road' from Isabelle, and to counter any new French paratroop drop. In the south the partial 304th Div (reinforced with a unit from 316th Div, artillery, mortars, and AAMGs) was to cut RP41, and suppress Isabelle's ability to intervene.

By this stage, the French defence was already constructed by mixing companies or even platoons of different units on some CRs; this reflected the character of the CEFEO, being intended to stiffen North Africans and Thais with paras or *légionnaires*. The use of scratch battle-groups for counter-attacks, which would become marked as the weeks passed, was largely due to casualties; on the other side, some amalgamations would also become necessary within decimated VPA regiments.

Major Dr Paul Grauwin, CO of 29 ACM. Together with Dr Jacques Gindrey's 44 ACM, this unit staffed the camp's dugout hospital north of the HQ area. Photos of Grauwin at work show him habitually stripped to the waist against the heat, and smoking a cigarette against the stink and the flies. Between them the two teams had a total of 26 personnel including four surgeons and six trained aides, who were assisted by volunteers from the camp's MP provost unit. The teams were equipped to triage casualties, operate on urgent cases, and stabilize them for evacuation. On the night of 13/14 March they had to carry out 51 major procedures; they were soon reinforced by the smaller 3 and 6 ACPs, but after the airfield closed on 28 March their task quickly became overwhelming. During late March two shell and 120mm mortar hits on the hospital itself killed 23 patients and wrecked the X-ray room. (Keystone-France/Gamma-Rapho via Getty Images)

Paras, probably of 1 BEP, making a counter-attack under mortar fire. This photo is believed to have been taken during the last week of March, during one of the combats to open the road down to CR Isabelle. (Keystone France/Gamma-Rapho via Getty Images)

When preparing for dusk attacks, the VPA artillery tried to leave enough time before nightfall to correct their fire, but too little time for French aircraft from the Delta to arrive. A major bombardment, particularly of the French artillery positions, started at 1715hrs on 30 March; it then switched briefly to the hill bastions and Dominique 3 for 1735–1738hrs, followed by creeping barrages on the approaches until infantry assaults began at about 1830hrs. In chronological order of the outcomes, the assaults were as follows.

Led by the usual skilled sappers to breach the wire, 215th Bn/98th Regt attacked Eliane 1, which was held by 3rd Co, I/4 RTM and a platoon from I/13 DBLE. The Moroccans fell back, and the hill was reported lost by 1925hrs.

The highest hill, Dominique 2, was more strongly defended by HQ, 10th and 11th Cos of III/3 RTA, plus a squad from 12th Co and Thai auxiliaries. After a close-range bombardment they were attacked by 166th and 154th Bns/209th Regt; at first the Algerians fought hard, but after they lost a trusted officer and were assaulted from two sides, they collapsed. Some surrendered, others fled, and the diehards of the French cadre were wiped out at about 2000hrs.

Dominique 1, held by half of 12th Co, III/3 RTA and by 4th Co, 5 BPVN, was also briefly but destructively bombarded, then assaulted on two axes by 16th and 428th Bns of 141st Regt. Again the wire was penetrated quickly, and the attackers made rapid progress; the defenders received little artillery support, the Algerians fell back, and GONO recorded the loss of the hill at 2150hrs. The weakly dug-in outpost of Dominique 6, between Dominiques 1 and 2, was untenable once the flanking hills had fallen. Nevertheless, the hard-driving Lt. Pham Van Phu kept his 2nd Co, 5 BPVN firing, making an orderly withdrawal only when 11th Bn/141st Regt threatened to overrun them at about 2200hrs.

Langlais ordered the tanks of Blue and Red platoons forward, and all night they moved up and down RP41 acting as mobile artillery between Dominique 3 and Eliane 2. Meanwhile, the Thais of 5th Co, BT 2 stuck bravely to their position on Dominique 5, firing on the enemy attacking the flanking hills, and then holding up 54th Bn/102nd Regt before it could link with the attackers of Dominique 3 west of the road.

Dominique 3 accomodated the howitzers of 4th Bty, II/4 RAC; the gunline was defended at the north by strongly wired-in parts of 12th and 9th Cos, III/3 RTA, and at the south by the rest of 9th Co. Giap had planned that it should be taken by 312th Div's 11th Bn/141st Regt and 115th Bn/165th Regt; these units should then link up with 54th Bn/102nd Regt from 308th Div, to overrun the reserve positions Elianes 10 and 12 on the riverside flats. But 115th Bn was pinned down in a minefield by French artillery, and only 11th Bn/141st Regt and 130th Bn/209th Regt reached the approaches to Dominique 3. (Its successful defence is described in the battlescene commentary on page 62.)

After taking Eliane 1 (see above), 215th Bn/98th Regt was supposed to advance at 2100hrs across a saddle to Eliane 4, which was held by HQ and 3rd Cos of 5 BPVN, plus 4th Co, 6 BPC. The assault troops were mauled by French shellfire, as were their support weapons on Eliane 1. By the time the survivors finally broke in at 0335hrs, at their sixth attempt, they had been reduced to platoon strength. From 0600hrs the shreds of 215th Bn withdrew, but the victory cost 5 BPVN 75 killed and wounded and 65 missing. (This unit's steadfastness had also been confirmed that night over on the west front, in the defence of Huguette 7 by its 1st Co against determined attacks by part of 36th Regt.)

The 'fifth hill', Eliane 2, was by far the most strongly fortified. The brick remains of the prewar district officer's station afforded artillery-proof cellars and bunkers, and roofed-over trenches linked positions into a coherent system. However, the south-east slope nicknamed 'Champs-Elysées' offered a clear path to the summit from wooded gullies around the base of the adjacent hill 'Baldy'. Patrol battles on 'Baldy' had prevented the VPA from digging approach trenches, but they began placing support weapons on it from about

Paras of a company HQ (note radio operator with SCR300) on one of the hilltop strongpoints – judging by its height, probably Dominique 2. On the first night of the 'Battle of the Five Hills', 30/31 March, both the 'high Dominiques' would be taken within little more than an hour by battalions from the VPA 209th and 141st Regts. (Keystone France/ Gamma-Rapho via Getty Images)

DEFENCE OF DOMINIQUE 3 BY 4TH BTY, II/4 RAC; C. 2230HRS, 30 MARCH 1954 (PP. 60–61)

Dominique 3 lay east of a 'dead elbow' of the river and west of RP41, covering the gap between the hill positions Dominique 1 and Dominique 2. At the outset of the 'Battle of the Five Hills' it was occupied by Lt. Paul Brunbrouck's 4th Bty, II/4 RAC, with four American M2A1 105mm howitzers. The gun line was protected by thick belts of wire and mines to the north and east, and defended by Lt. Filaudeau's dug-in 9/ and 12/III/3 RTA.

After a brief VPA bombardment, Dominique 2 – held by part of III/3 RTA – fell to infantry assault by about 2030hrs on 30 March; on Dominique 1, 11/III/3 RTA and 4/5 BPVN were overrun by about 2150hrs. Survivors soon sought shelter in Dominique 3, but when Brunbrouck reported the fall of both hills to his battalion commander, he was not believed. Dominique 3 now blocked an otherwise open path to the river, and by about 2200hrs it began to come under infantry attack, initially by 130th Bn/209th Inf Regt and later, from 0300hrs, by 11th Bn/141st Inf Regt, both from 312th Div.

Lt. Brunbrouck conducted a stubborn defence; during the seven-hour fight that followed he was twice ordered by Lt.-Col. Langlais to disable his guns and pull his men out, but he refused. Although one gun was disabled, only half a dozen gunners were wounded and none killed. Often obliged to fire zero-delay shells at point blank range, 4th Bty and its Algerian infantry defenders repelled repeated attacks until after 0500hrs. During that night each crew of 4th Bty fired about 450 rounds.

* * *

Most night actions at Dien Bien Phu were illuminated by *luciolle* parachute flares. The gunpits were about 30 feet across; the edge of the circle around which the gun was physically traversed by 'capstan' rotation of the trail legs was reinforced with empty

shell cases driven into the ground. Dug into the earth walls, timber-and-sandbag stowage bays for ammunition had only the shallowest overhead cover. A trench led off from each gunpit to join a sunken lane behind, which linked the four gun positions, the main ammunition and personnel shelters, and the battery command dugout.

Served by a French NCO gun captain and West African crewmen, this howitzer is shown at the moment of maximum recoil, as an empty shell case is ejected. The regulation crew was eight men, but that night some gunners were detached to reinforce the Algerian infantrymen in close defence. The immediate crew were the gun captain (**1**), responsible for elevation and firing; the gunlayer (**2**), controlling the traverse; and the loader (**3**), who was fed shells by two ammunition numbers (e.g. **4**). At need, shells were carried up (**5**) from the battery's central ammo dump. Clear of the gun, two men (**6** and **7**) adjusted the fuzes of the shells as ordered, using the M26 fuze-setter. Out of the picture to the left, another man first adjusted charges – removing from the case of the semi-fixed round the instructed number of its seven bagged propellant charges. In action, gunpits quickly became cluttered with 'empty brass' and packing materials (and sometimes, more dangerously, with discarded charge bags).

The gun crew wear olive-green M1947/52 'all arms' *treillis de combat* fatigues, and American M1 helmets (**8**). Brunbrouck (**9**) is identified by his Colonial Artillery *calot* cap. Paul Brunbrouck was a cool but charismatic leader who earned the devotion of his gunners. This action earned him the Legion of Honour; to the great distress of his men, he would be mortally wounded by counter-battery fire on the main artillery position on 13 April.

On both sides, 120mm heavy mortars played an important part throughout the battle; although lacking delay or airburst fuzes, their 41-pound bombs were as destructive as 105mm shells. This photo shows a crew of the Legion's CEPML firing a 'bedding-in' shot late in Operation *Castor*, when Muong Thanh village was still largely intact. On 13 March GONO had 28 of these weapons; by 16 March eight had been destroyed and would never be replaced. The VPA started the battle with 20 at most – as in almost all heavy weapon categories, their assumed superiority in numbers is a mistake. (ullstein-bild via Getty Images)

1800hrs, to join the mortars, MGs, and RCLs planted on 'Phoney' hill north-east of Eliane 2. On 30/31 March, Eliane 2 was held by the HQ and two rifle companies of I/4 RTM, two platoons from I/13 DBLE, and 1st Co, I BEP. Over on Eliane 4, Maj. Bigeard waited to orchestrate reinforcements.

The initial bombardment from 1720 to 1820hrs caused damage and French casualties; but a telephone wire cut by French counter-shelling left 174th Regt's CO without orders, and after the barrage lifted he delayed the advance of his 249th and 251st Bns from 'Baldy'. They were badly punished by French artillery tree-bursts, and then by enfilading fire from Eliane 3 and the quad-.50-cals in Junon. When their assault up 'Champs-Elysées' finally began at 1945hrs, the heads of the two columns bunched up only about 30 yards apart, presenting easy targets. Under murderous fire, they soon lost contact with their regimental HQ.

Even so, by 2300hrs 2nd Co, I/4 RTM had been forced up the slope; but when their transverse trench was assaulted, the defenders disappeared into the underground bunkers and tunnels. The uniquely robust overhead cover allowed French artillery to fire on Eliane 2 without causing French casualties, and the infantry then emerged to counter-attack the weakened and dazed attackers. These unanticipated tactics caused the VPA heavy losses, and some bafflement. (Repeated over the following nights by companies rotated onto the hill, they would continue to save Eliane 2.)

The 174th Regt's 255th Bn was thrown forward in reinforcement, but by now the VPA support weapons on 'Baldy' had been silenced and others had run out of ammunition. By midnight, Maj. Bigeard had sent in two more companies of 1 BEP, and 255th Bn's attack was foiled by repeating the previous tactics. By 0430hrs 249th and 251st Bns were both so mauled that they had retreated, and the 255th Bn was only clinging to the bottom of 'Champs-Elysées'. Subsequent counter-attacks by 4th Co, 1 BEP, plus a scratch Legion-and-Thai company and Red Ptn's tanks, cleared the slope by 1130hrs on the 31st.

SECOND ASSAULT PHASE OPENS, 30/31 MARCH 1954

The 'Battle of the Five Hills' opened on the night of 30/31 March with ambitious simultaneous VPA assaults on all the 'high' Dominique and Eliane positions, and one 'low' strongpoint behind them. Had all been taken, GONO's immediate survival would have demanded very costly counter-attacks, which might well have failed – despite the fact that at this stage of the battle Giap ordered that captured features be held only weakly, since he feared French artillery and aircraft more than counter-attacks. In the event, although Dominiques 1 and 2 and Eliane 1 fell that first night, an understrength VPA follow-through at Eliane 4, and a reinforced French defence of the uniquely strong Eliane 2, saved both. Over the next three nights, Giap sacrificed a number of his assault battalions, and used up most of his artillery ammunition, in failed repetitions of the same tactics – and ten days later, Eliane 1 would be recaptured by 6 BPC.

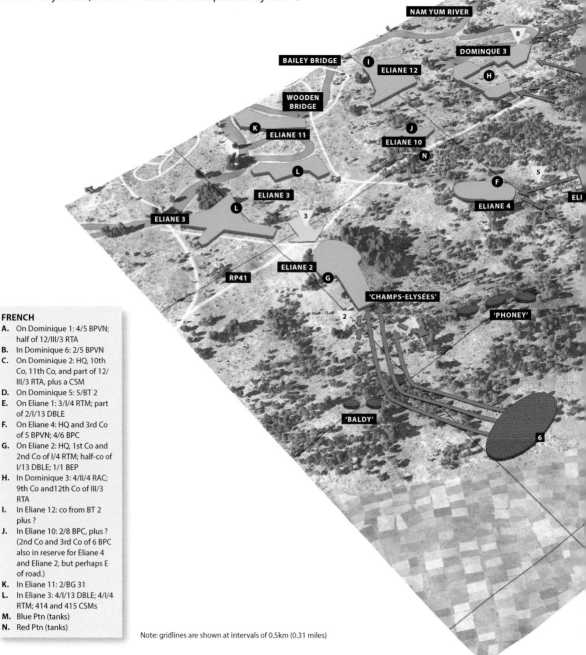

NAM YUM RIVER

BAILEY BRIDGE

WOODEN BRIDGE

DOMINQUE 3

ELIANE 12

ELIANE 11

ELIANE 10

ELIANE 3

ELIANE 3

ELIANE 4

ELIANE 2

RP41

'CHAMPS-ELYSÉES'

'PHONEY'

'BALDY'

ELI

FRENCH

A. On Dominique 1: 4/5 BPVN; half of 12/III/3 RTA
B. In Dominique 6: 2/5 BPVN
C. On Dominique 2: HQ, 10th Co, 11th Co, and part of 12/III/3 RTA, plus a CSM
D. On Dominique 5: 5/BT 2
E. On Eliane 1: 3/I/4 RTM; part of 2/I/13 DBLE
F. On Eliane 4: HQ and 3rd Co of 5 BPVN; 4/6 BPC
G. On Eliane 2: HQ, 1st Co and 2nd Co of I/4 RTM; half-co of I/13 DBLE; 1/1 BEP
H. In Dominique 3: 4/II/4 RAC; 9th Co and 12th Co of III/3 RTA
I. In Eliane 12: co from BT 2 plus ?
J. In Eliane 10: 2/8 BPC, plus ? (2nd Co and 3rd Co of 6 BPC also in reserve for Eliane 4 and Eliane 2, but perhaps E of road.)
K. In Eliane 11: 2/BG 31
L. In Eliane 3: 4/I/13 DBLE; 4/I/4 RTM; 414 and 415 CSMs
M. Blue Ptn (tanks)
N. Red Ptn (tanks)

Note: gridlines are shown at intervals of 0.5km (0.31 miles)

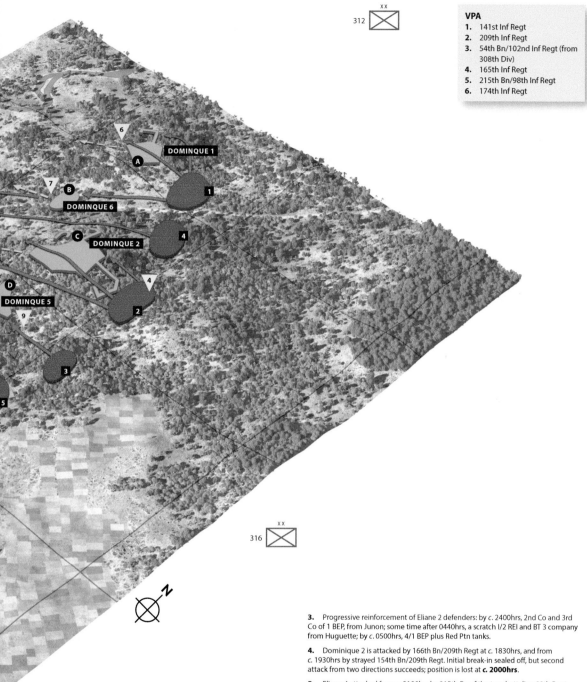

312 ⊠ xx

VPA
1. 141st Inf Regt
2. 209th Inf Regt
3. 54th Bn/102nd Inf Regt (from 308th Div)
4. 165th Inf Regt
5. 215th Bn/98th Inf Regt
6. 174th Inf Regt

DOMINQUE 1

A

6

1

7

B

DOMINQUE 6

C

DOMINQUE 2

4

D

DOMINQUE 5

4

2

9

3

5

316 ⊠ xx

N

EVENTS

Note: key timings are provided in bold. All events take place between 30 and 31 March.

1. Assaults begin, those on initial objectives all with close support from 75mm guns and mortars. Eliane 1, attacked from c. 1830hrs by 215th Bn/98th Regt, falls at **c. 1925hrs**.

2. Eliane 2 is attacked from c. 1945hrs by 249th and 251st Bns/174th Regt, at first supported by heavy weapons on 'Phoney' and 'Baldy'. Pushed to top of 'Champs-Elysées' corridor by c. 2300hrs, defenders shelter in bunkers under own artillery fire. By c. 2400hrs attackers reinforced by 255th Bn/174th Regt; by **c. 0430hrs** weakened 249th and 251st Bns are withdrawn, and 255th Bn holds only foot of 'Champs-Elysées'.

3. Progressive reinforcement of Eliane 2 defenders: by c. 2400hrs, 2nd Co and 3rd Co of 1 BEP, from Junon; some time after 0440hrs, a scratch I/2 REI and BT 3 company from Huguette; by c. 0500hrs, 4/1 BEP plus Red Ptn tanks.

4. Dominique 2 is attacked by 166th Bn/209th Regt at c. 1830hrs, and from c. 1930hrs by strayed 154th Bn/209th Regt. Initial break-in sealed off, but second attack from two directions succeeds; position is lost at **c. 2000hrs**.

5. Eliane 4 attacked from c. 2100hrs by 215th Bn of the two-battalion 98th Regt. Already tired from capture of Eliane 1, this unit is virtually destroyed in repeated attacks; survivors gain small foothold at c. 0335hrs, but withdrawn from **c. 0600hrs**.

6. Dominique 1 attacked from two directions at c. 1830hrs by 16th and 148th Bns/141st Regt; hill is lost **c. 2150hrs**.

7. Dominique 6 defenders fire in support of Dominiques 1 and 2: withdraw **c. 2200hrs** under attack by 11th Bn/141st Regt.

8. Dominique 3 attacked from c. 2200hrs by 130th Bn/209th Regt, and later by 11th Bn/141st Regt; identity of attackers of southern position unclear, but all attacks repulsed, and cease **c. 0500hrs**. The 115th Bn/165th Regt stopped north of Dominique 3 by mines and artillery before it can engage.

9. Defenders of Dominique 5 repulse attack at **c. 2300hrs** by 54th Bn/102nd Regt (from 308th Div).

Anticipating the requested drop of II/1 RCP on 31 March, Lt.-Col. Langlais planned an immediate response. From Isabelle, DZ 'Sonia' south of Eliane 2 was to be cleared by III/3 REI, part of BT 3, and the tank platoon, which would then press on to capture 'Baldy'. Meanwhile, Eliane 1 would be retaken by 6 BPC, and Dominique 2 by 8 BPC.

The Isabelle force advanced north at 0700hrs, but after a see-saw battle with parts of all three battalions of 57th Regt it was forced to withdraw at 1150hrs. The failure to clear the DZ was immaterial, however: after repeated arguments, Hanoi refused to drop the extra para battalion that day. The delayed 8 BPC attempt on Dominique 2 was locally successful, but ultimately failed. That on Eliane 1 by 6 BPC succeeded in taking the summit at high cost, but the furious paras eventually had to withdraw: without the arrival of II/1 RCP to relieve them, the hill could not be held.

* * *

The above account gives the flavour of the fighting during the first night of the 'Battle of the Five Hills'. For reasons of space, the essentials of the nights that followed must be summarized more briefly.

On 31 March/1 April only Eliane 2 was seriously attacked: by 18th Bn from 308th Div's 102nd Regt, marched laboriously 4 miles across from the west, and by part of 174th Regt. The assault was delayed until 2230hrs; the defending two companies, of I/4 RTM and 6 BPC, adopted the same tactics as on the previous night, and were reinforced by a company each from 6 and 8 BPC and half of 2nd Co, I/13 DBLE. Once again, the VPA reached the top of 'Champs-Elysées', but, under shellfire, were unable to locate the entrances to the underground bunkers. Both tank platoons supported counter-attacks, but 'Bazeille' was immobilized; thereafter this tank would serve as a static pillbox in several later actions.

In the north-west, the isolated Huguette 7 was partly lost to 36th Regt, but retaken with artillery support. The next night the attack was repeated; now defended by only 40 *légionnaires* from I/2 REI, the position was lost, and a dawn counter-attack failed. Also on 1/2 April, parts of 1 BEP defeated

Here photographed in 1996, WO Aristide Carette's M24 'Bazeille' was abandoned on the summit of Eliane 2 in the early hours of 1 April, when the third of three 'bazooka' or RCL hits caused a serious engine fire. (This spelling of the tank's name, without the usual final 's', is used throughout Gen. Mengelle's memoir of 3/1 RCC's part in the battle.) The placing of the .50-cal. MG identifies the squadron's Blue Ptn; before 'Bazeille' was knocked out, two sergeants of 1 BEP had been riding the tank and manning the MG during a counter-attack. The Chaffee continued to be used as a static pillbox until Eliane 2 finally fell early on the morning of 7 May. (Photo courtesy Kieran Lynch)

The northern Huguettes, 30 March–18 April 1954

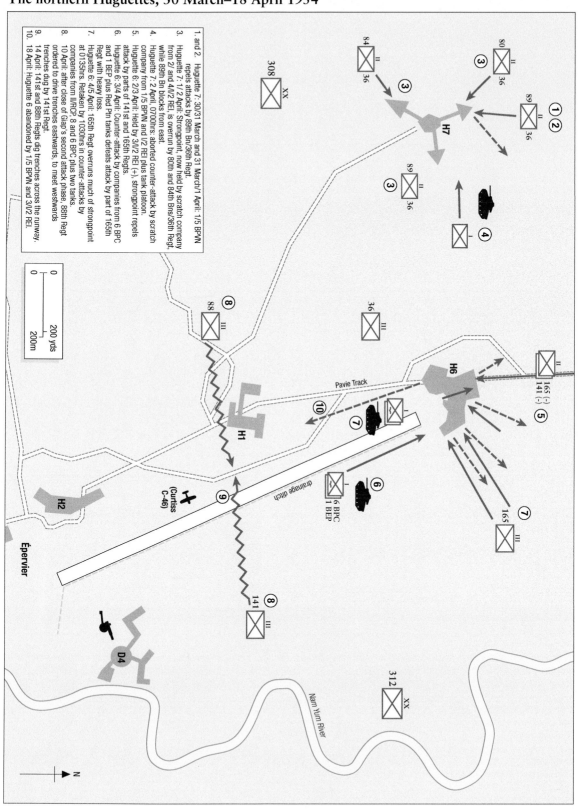

1. and 2. Huguette 7: 30/31 March and 31 March/1 April: 1/5 BPVN repels attacks by 89th Bn/36th Regt.

3. Huguette 7: 1/2 April: Strongpoint, now held by scratch company from 2/ and 4/I/2 REI, is overrun by 80th and 84th Bns/36th Regt.

4. Huguette 7: 2 April, 0700hrs: aborted counter-attack by scratch company from 1/5 BPVN and I/2 REI plus tank platoon.

5. Huguette 6: 2/3 April: Held by 3/I/2 REI (+), strongpoint repels attack by parts of 141st and 165th Regts.

6. Huguette 6: 3/4 April: Counter-attack by companies from 6 BPC and 1 BEP plus Red Ptn tanks defeats attack by part of 165th Regt with heavy loss.

7. Huguette 6: 4/5 April: 165th Regt overruns much of strongpoint at 0135hrs. Retaken by 1030hrs in counter-attacks by companies from II/RCP, 8 and 6 BPC plus two tanks.

8. 10 April: after close of Giap's second attack phase, 88th Regt ordered to drive trenches eastwards, to meet westwards trenches dug by 141st Regt.

9. 14 April: 141st and 88th Regts dig trenches across the runway.

10. 18 April: Huguette 6 abandoned by 1/5 BPVN and 3/I/2 REI.

0 — 200 yds
0 — 200m

308 XX

84 II 36
80 II 36
89 II 36
89 II 36
③ ③ ③ ① ②
④
H7

88 III
36 III
165 (-) II
141 (-) II
⑧ ⑤

H6
Pavie Track
⑩ ⑦
6 BPC
1 BEP
⑥
165 III
⑦

H1
(Curtiss
C-46)
⑨
drainage ditch
141 III
⑧

H2

Épervier

D4

312 XX

Nam Yum River

N

another attempt on Eliane 2 by scratch companies from the weakened 18th Bn/102nd Regt.

During that night the first small element of II/1 RCP was parachuted in, with difficulty. Only six men from each 'stick' could jump during each pass over the reduced DZ, and since these 'Banjo' drops could not be made while *luciole* air-dropped flares were vitally illuminating the ground fighting, they were often disrupted.

The loss of Huguette 7 demoralized the Thai auxiliaries in Françoise, which would be abandoned after they deserted during the day of 2 April. Morning counter-attacks on Eliane 2 cleared all but a handful of the enemy from 'Champs-Elysées', and on the night of 2/3 April the paras of 1 BEP drove back yet another attack by a cobbled-together force from 102nd Regt, using the familiar tactics of sheltering underground from French artillery support. After suffering the equivalent of a battalion and a half destroyed (890 casualties) on Eliane 2 alone, the VPA's ranks were already being filled out with raw replacements. That night effectively ended for the time being the fighting for the Five Hills, but not the second assault phase.

A paratrooper cares for a comrade after a counter-attack. On the Five Hills such missions were carried out by one or two companies at a time from 1 BEP, 6 and 8 BPC, 2 REI, and 13 DBLE, often supported by one of the tank platoons. The VPA learned the hard way to have great respect for French counter-attacks, and Giap's briefings for the later May Day assaults stressed the threat they posed. (ullstein bild via Getty Images)

Giap now switched his focus to Huguette 6, isolated at the end of the airstrip. On 2/3 April it was successfully defended by a company of I/2 REI plus a platoon of Béatrice survivors from III/13 DBLE. Shockingly, however, on 3 April some of the latter deserted after being confronted by the VPA with a display of mutilated French corpses.

Famous photo of paratroop commanders during a daily conference in Lt.-Col. Langlais' HQ: (left to right) Capt. André Botella (5 BPVN), Maj. Marcel Bigeard (6 BPC), Capt. Pierre Tourret (8 BPC), Lt.-Col. Pierre Langlais (GAP 2, later GONO chief of operations), and Maj. Hubert de Séguins-Pazzis (who succeeded Langlais in command of GAP 2). Absent are Maj. Jean Bréchignac (II/1 RCP) and Maj. Maurice Guiraud (1 BEP, later BMEP). (Bettmann Archive via Getty Images)

Early on 4 April a promising attack by 165th Regt from 312th Div left a claimed 500 casualties on the field after it was caught and destroyed in the open by a tank-led counter-attack by three companies from 6 BPC and 1 BEP, and French aircraft. That night most of II/1 RCP parachuted in, and the unit would be completed on 5/6 April.

On 4/5 April all three battalions of 165th Regt assaulted Huguette 6 from 0030hrs, and overran most of it. However, the position was retaken by 1030hrs on the 5th in successive counter-attacks by companies from 8 BPC, II/1 RCP, and 6 BPC with tank support. The French lost 221 casualties, but again inflicted heavy VPA losses.

This brought Giap's second, and extremely costly offensive phase to an unavoidable close. He had expended most of his artillery ammunition and the lives of a significant proportion of the eight infantry regiments he had committed, and the morale of their survivors was approaching collapse.

STRANGLEHOLD AND ATTRITION: 8–30 APRIL

During this month the character of the fighting reverted to siege warfare; Col. de Castries called it 'a bit like Verdun … but without the Sacred Way'. Both attackers and defenders laboured constantly with pick and shovel, under intermittent shell and mortar fire, and took losses when repelling or mounting trench raids. The medical care provided for the escalating numbers of wounded on both sides was increasingly inadequate. Some French companies were down to perhaps 80 men each, and had to be amalgamated (e.g. in I/13 DBLE, 5 BPVN, and 6 and 8 BPC). Both sides had to absorb their reinforcements, and rebuild their essential stores. The garrison would receive fewer than 1,000 of the former, and dwindling quantities of the latter, due to the multiple difficulties of parachuting men and supplies in the face of AA fire and nightly shelling. Meanwhile, GONO's pleas for effective tactical air support would continue to be disappointed.

French reinforcements would be limited to one battalion – the Legion's 2 BEP, dropped between 10 and 12 April. Replacements for existing units were dropped piecemeal, at an average of about 50 per night. Since 5/6 April individual non-airborne volunteers had been jumping in after only the most rudimentary ground-training; landing injuries proved no more frequent than

The C-119 Packet heavy transport could slide 6-ton loads out of its 'clam-shell' tail doors in a single pass, in contrast to the C-47 Dakota's 2½ tons manhandled awkwardly out of a side door during several passes. (This advantage became a drawback when loads, particularly of 105mm shells, with the latest delay or airburst fuzes, were misdropped to the VPA.) Although GATAC/Nord eventually had 29 C-119s during April, it was chronically short of trained aircrews – for most of the battle, only six French plus 12 American. The former sometimes had to be recalled at short notice to fly Dakotas, and the latter – provided by the CIA – were officially forbidden from flying 'combat missions' (though they often did). The one C-119 shot down was flown by American pilots, James B. McGovern and Wallace Buford. (SeM/ Universal Images Group via Getty Images)

Portrait of a prisoner taken during the fighting; most VPA infantry now had these quilted jackets, and were glad of them, especially after the arrival of the monsoon rains – intermittent from 29 March, and non-stop from 25 April. When rotated to the jungle camps in the rear, the men slept on the ground with only a bamboo mat, or banana leaves laid on a plastic sheet. Malaria was also endemic in the siege army, which had very few mosquito nets, and very little quinine – the *bo doi* had to share it in almost homeopathic doses. (Keystone France/Gamma-Rapho via Getty Images)

among paras, since all were now landing haphazardly all over the camp. By the end of the battle at least 1,800 of these extraordinarily courageous men had jumped into the nighttime chaos of Dien Bien Phu. Few can have had any illusions about their probable fate, and about 25 per cent of them are believed to have been non-Europeans.

Dropping of ammunition and other essentials became increasingly difficult as the perimeter tightened, and from 7 April the flak persuaded the Air Force to drop Dakota-loads from no lower than 8,500 feet. (With much greater capacity and big tail doors that emptied them quickly, C-119s continued to make their single passes from much lower.) The improvised delayed-opening devices which the Air Force adopted never worked reliably, and increasing amounts of stores – particularly precious 105mm shells, complete with the latest bunker-busting delay fuses – fell either behind VPA lines or simply out of reach. Although only three C-47s were actually shot down over Dien Bien Phu, many returned to Hanoi riddled with holes, sometimes with wounded and burned crewmen. Having to make repeated straight-and-level passes in the face of AA fire put an increasingly serious strain on the pilots, not all of whom could stand it.

While night patrol activity by both sides continued, Giap issued orders to all his divisions to tighten their encirclement and approach trenches around the remaining French positions, in preparation for renewed assaults on the Huguettes on 15 April. (From 8 April, the individual company strongpoints Huguette 4 and Claudines 1 and 2 were transformed into a new CR, Liliane, for I/4 RTM. Huguettes 5 and 6 were now held by parts of I/2 REI and 5 BPVN; Huguettes 1 and 3, by parts of I/2 REI; and Huguette 2 by the remnant of III/13 DBLE.) In the event, however, the next major action was unexpected: the French recapture of Eliane 1 on 10 April.

Eliane 1 was held by a single company from 938th Bn/98th Regt, reinforced too late by half a company from 439th Bn. Although 6 BPC had been reduced to about 240 men, Bigeard's plan for its assault gave it powerful support, including heavy fire and smoke-shells on the flanking Dominiques. A preparatory shoot by 105s and 120mm mortars opened at 0600hrs, and the paras advanced from Eliane 4 at 0645hrs, closely following a creeping barrage. Despite 48 casualties, they took the summit (but not the far slope) by 0800hrs, secured it at 1130hrs, and were relieved on it at 1400hrs by half of II/1 RCP. A VPA counter-attack on 11 April was driven off.

This success lifted GONO's morale, but any hopes of exploiting it were dashed on 11/12 April, when a major counter-attack by 98th Regt and part of 209th Regt was only thrown back with difficulty by parts of II/1 RCP, 1 BEP, and 5 BPVN. The eastern slope of Eliane 1 remained in the hands of 888th Bn/176th Regt (brought all the way up from Isabelle – again, Giap's shifting of units from the west and south to patch his two divisions on the east speaks of their heavy losses).

Although 351st Div's artillery ammunition had to be strictly rationed until resupply arrived, the focus remained on the northern Huguettes. At

the far end of the airstrip, Huguette 6 was held by 1/5 BPVN and 3/I/2 REI, and the other strongpoints by the rest of I/2 REI and the rebuilt company of III/13 DBLE. Now totalling no more than a battalion equivalent, these men faced four (if understrength) VPA regiments. While the weakened 165th Regt from 312th Div tightened its grip around Huguette 6, 141st Regt was to drive trenches towards the runway from the east; simultaneously, 308th Div's 36th and 88th Regts, respectively above and below Huguette 1, were to dig from west to east.

Fighting centred directly or indirectly on the nightly resupply parties carrying ammo and water up to Huguette 6, via the Pavie Track or the runway and drainage ditch; these were typically escorted by paras and tanks, and protected by flanking ambushes. Both sides had some successes, but the link became harder to maintain; three parallel trenches soon blocked the way south of Huguette 1. Early on 14 April the first small trench was cut right across the runway between Huguettes 1 and 2, and later that day a tank-led attempt to break through failed. That night Legion paras reached Huguette 6; but fierce fighting by both night and day until the morning of 16 April dragged in parts of 1 and 2 BEP, 6 and 8 BPC, and I and III/13 DBLE, requiring tank and considerable artillery support. Movement now depended on a long 'Métro' of communication trenches roofed over with PSP – and the vagaries of the morning fog.

On 17 April Giap ordered up another 4,000 replacements and put a further 1,000 on standby. That night a failed attempt to reach and withdraw the Huguette 6 garrison cost 1 BEP some 100 casualties; but a separate action allowed the installation on the 18th of strongpoint Opéra facing Huguette 1 from the east. Giap planned to eliminate Huguette 6 on 20 April; however, under cover of fog on the morning of the 18th the remaining fit survivors

VPA troops feeding in one of the jungle camps surrounding Dien Bien Phu. Rations had improved since February (when some had had to forage in the jungle for edible green stuff), but became less reliable again after the rains started. They usually consisted of rice, salt, beansprouts, and sometimes a little dried fish, buffalo or 'bush meat', as well as an issue of tobacco. (SeM Studio/Fototeca/Universal Images Group via Getty Images)

broke out down the runway, and about 60 of them made it. (They had been forced to abandon their wounded, including a last heroic Legion machine-gunner who gave covering fire until he was killed.)

Since all French cargo and paratroop drops took place from south to north, the loss of Huguette 6 meant that AAMGs would now enjoy positions allowing them to shoot straight into the faces of approaching Dakota pilots.

On 18 and 19 April 4/I/13 DBLE was installed (only slowly, and with difficulty) to take over Huguette 1. Surrounded by open ground, this position was strongly wired and had internal obstacles, making a conventional assault particularly risky. The 36th Regt therefore changed their tactics: they largely abandoned digging approach trenches and started actually tunnelling (which could be carried out around the clock), while positioning support weapons and snipers, and secretly cutting the French wire by night. Although numbers of men had to be assigned to bailing in the shallow, waterlogged tunnels, this paid dividends on 22/23 April. After the briefest bombardment, assault parties infiltrated the perimeter by three tunnels (parts of 80th, 84th, and 89th Bns from the west, north, and south respectively). The western and northern companies quickly established footholds and brought up heavy weapons, followed by the 89th Bn element. The regimental commander had to abandon the tunnels to flooding and commit every man he had to exploit the break-ins, but Huguette 1 fell by about 0230hrs. The trench system south of it was quickly reinforced by 88th Regt, with the 102nd in reserve, and the tunnelling method was recommended throughout the siege army.

The loss of Huguette 1 made Opéra untenable, and further reduced the available DZ for all future air-drops. Brigadier-General de Castries insisted on an immediate counter-attack to retake it, despite Langlais' unwillingness to commit his only true reserve (2 BEP, already reduced to 350 men). When

its long journey across from the Elianes was spotted, it came under fire, and Giap warned his artillery and mortars for massed shoots. Bigeard planned an unprecedentedly heavy airstrike on Huguette 1 at 1345hrs, to be followed by an artillery bombardment at 1400–1410hrs. Protected by smoke north and south, 7 and 8/2 BEP would then thrust west from Opéra while 5 and 6/2 BEP would come up from Huguette 2 to attack from the south; the Legion paras would be supported by 'Douaumont' and 'Mulhouse', the only operational tanks available.

Through notorious failures of communications and command-and-control, the operation failed dismally. It took 2 BEP much longer to reach their jumping-off positions than anticipated; the air strike was successful, but a half-hour delay then allowed VPA reinforcement before 7th and 8th Cos assaulted, and heavy MG and artillery fire then pinned them down in the open. Despite the tanks' supporting fire, 5th Co's advance was blocked in trenches around the wrecked Curtiss C-46 just south of Huguette 1, and 6th Co never engaged at all. Resuming control from 2 BEP's Maj. Liesenfelt perhaps at about 1500hrs (the sources are contradictory), Bigeard ordered the paras to fall

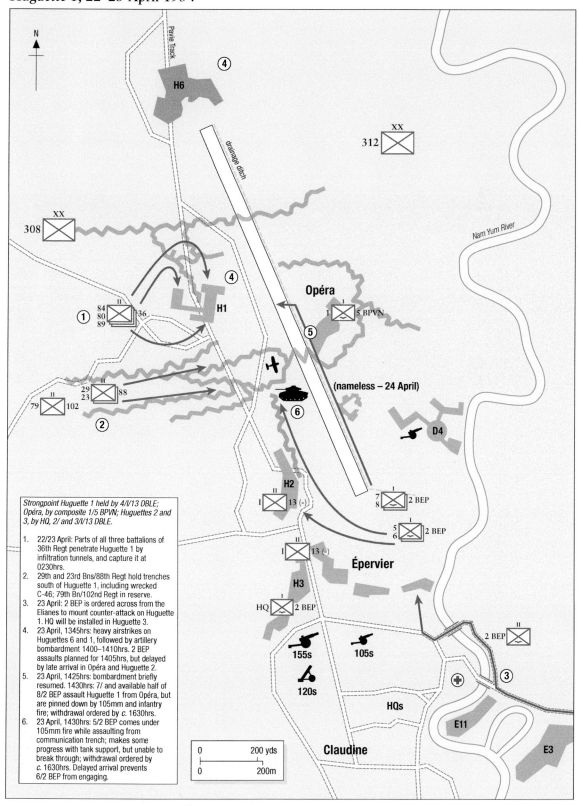

N

Pavie Track

H6

④

drainage ditch

312   XX

308   XX

④

H1

84
80   II   36
89

①

Opéra

1   I   5 BPVN

⑤

(nameless – 24 April)

29   II
23   88

79   II   102

②

⑥

D4

H2

I   II   13 (-)

7   I   2 BEP
8

5   I   2 BEP
6

II   13 (-)

Épervier

H3

HQ   I   2 BEP

2 BEP   II

155s   105s

120s

HQs

③

E11

E3

**Strongpoint Huguette 1 held by 4/I/13 DBLE;
Opéra, by composite 1/5 BPVN; Huguettes 2 and
3, by HQ, 2/ and 3/I/13 DBLE.**

1. 22/23 April: Parts of all three battalions of
    36th Regt penetrate Huguette 1 by
    infiltration tunnels, and capture it at
    0230hrs.
2. 29th and 23rd Bns/88th Regt hold trenches
    south of Huguette 1, including wrecked
    C-46; 79th Bn/102nd Regt in reserve.
3. 23 April: 2 BEP is ordered across from the
    Elianes to mount counter-attack on Huguette
    1. HQ will be installed in Huguette 3.
4. 23 April, 1345hrs: heavy airstrikes on
    Huguettes 6 and 1, followed by artillery
    bombardment 1400–1410hrs. 2 BEP
    assaults planned for 1405hrs, but delayed
    by late arrival in Opéra and Huguette 2.
5. 23 April, 1425hrs: bombardment briefly
    resumed. 1430hrs: 7/ and available half of
    8/2 BEP assault Huguette 1 from Opéra, but
    are pinned down by 105mm and infantry
    fire; withdrawal ordered by c. 1630hrs.
6. 23 April, 1430hrs: 5/2 BEP comes under
    105mm fire while assaulting from
    communication trench; makes some
    progress with tank support, but unable to
    break through; withdrawal ordered by
    c. 1630hrs. Delayed arrival prevents
    6/2 BEP from engaging.

Nam Yum River

0   200 yds
0   200m

Claudine

73

FINAL DEFENCE OF ELIANE 1 BY II/1 RCP; C. 2200HRS, 1 MAY 1954 (PP. 74–75)

The whole position had been under intermittent fire since 10 April, and trenches were unstable under the monsoon rains; on the previous night the paratroopers had attempted to rebuild parapets with earth-sacks made of *cai phen*. Much of the inadequate barbed wire had already been destroyed, and some VPA approach trenches reached to within ten yards of what was left.

The assault was made by two battalions, 439th from 98th Regt and 888th from 176th Regt. When it began at about 2020hrs, following a short bombardment, Eliane 1 was held by Lt. Périou's 1/II/1 RCP (the battalion's former 22 CIPLE before integration in October 1953). From its 114 all ranks, only 17 (not including Yves Périou) survived the action and the subsequent withdrawal to Eliane 4. They were reinforced first by Lt. Leguére's 80-strong 3rd/4th Co (merged since 12 April), which was reduced to 25 men during this action, and at 2200hrs by part of Capt. Cledic's 2nd Co. Although pushed back from the summit to the reverse slope, the paras continued to resist for several hours before the survivors were ordered to withdraw over the saddle to Eliane 4, and Eliane 1 was recorded as lost at 0200hrs.

Of 667 all ranks of II/1 RCP who had jumped into the camp over the nights of 1/2 to 5/6 April, 238 are believed to have survived the battle and the captivity that followed.

* * *

This battalion seem to have been almost completely clothed in TAP camouflage smocks and trousers. The web equipment was, again, TAP M1950, with US M1943 folding entrenching-tools tucked behind belts. The officer (**1**) has a US luminous disc fixed to the back of his helmet for night-time recognition. The zigzag trench allows a squad's LMG team (**2**) to rake the charging enemy obliquely with their FM24/29. Personal weapons are the usual mixture of US carbines, CR39 rifles and MAT49 SMGs, with US Mk II, and French DF37 fragmentation grenades (**3**).

Apart from this battalion's favoured US-camouflage 'fisherman's hat', figure (**4**) is speculative. An unknown number of night-sniper M3 carbines fitted with bulky optical sights and infra-red projectors, linked to slung battery packs, had been supplied to GONO. Also, on 28/29 April, some 300 US 'flak jackets' were air-dropped. Most went to artillery and mortar crews, but some to paratroopers – particularly in II/1 RCP, whose 3rd/4th Co reportedly had significant numbers; snipers and weapon crews supposedly got priority. We follow a French source in speculating that these were the 1945 Armor Vest M12 (which was certainly supplied to the French *Bataillon de Corée* with US 2nd Inf Div in Korea.)

The *bo doi* of 98th Inf Regt probably wore uniforms of varying green and khaki drab shades due to dispersed manufacture, with quilted jackets, and woven-rattan helmets with hessian and string-net covers. On this occasion they are described as wearing white gauze 'smog masks', for reasons that are unclear (**5**). Small arms were typically captured French MAS36 or supplied Chinese Type 24 Mauser rifles, with plentiful Chinese Type 50 SMGs (**5**) and stick-grenades. Usually, separate companies were fed into attacks successively, preceded by sappers with bangalores and satchel charges (**6**). The standard platoon attack formation was in columns of three-man fire-teams, led by an LMG (the Czech-designed, Chinese-made ZB26, called by the French the 'Skoda'). They might be supported by 57mm RCLs devolved from the regimental 'infantry gun' company.

SB2C-5 Helldiver of the *Aéronavale* 3rd Flotilla from the carrier *Arromanches*, operating from an airfield in the Delta. The naval fighter and bomber crews were respected for their high work rate, and paid for it: three F6F Hellcats of 11th Flotilla, two of the Helldivers, and two four-engined PB4Y-2 Privateers of 28th Flotilla were shot down over Dien Bien Phu between 15 March and 7/8 May 1954. The Privateers' eight-man crews represented many of the total of 21 Navy flyers who were lost over Dien Bien Phu or died in captivity. (Keystone France/Gamma-Rapho via Getty Images)

back, which was only accomplished at the cost of further losses. In all the battalion suffered 95 casualties; Liesenfelt was blamed, but Bigeard later admitted that he shared the responsibility.

On 24 April the two Legion para units were merged into a strong composite Foreign Parachute Marching Battalion (BMEP) under 1 BEP's Maj. Guiraud. The company of mixed survivors holding Opéra withdrew south down the drainage ditch, and reinstalled themselves in a waterlogged 'nameless strongpoint'.

The tactical air support always had to be parcelled out between hunting VPA artillery, direct strikes against infantry, and suppressing the flak. In protest against the inadequacy of the latter effort, the American C-119 crews went on strike from 24 to 30 April, and would never resume low-level missions. On 25 April the monsoon rains began in earnest, flooding the main

While they knocked out some AA guns in late March, the B-26s (A-26 Invaders) of the two under-trained bomber squadrons in the Delta generally failed to support GONO effectively. They were short of both aircrews and mechanics, and had an availability deficit of around 40 per cent. Their former transport aircrews suffered from the lack of an experienced bomber commander, inadequate briefings, and the absence of effective forward air control from the ground. They only carried about half their bombload capacity, and the bomb fuzes were often incorrectly set. Two Invaders were shot down, both on 26 April, by 37mm fire at up to 9,000 feet altitude. In all, Air Force aircrew lost in action over Dien Bien Phu or died in captivity totalled about 36 men. (Bettmann Archive via Getty Images)

camp and Isabelle and preventing much aerial activity. Four days later the garrison was put on half-rations.

Infantry strength was now recorded at 5,500 men, but 1,400 of those were pointlessly stranded in Isabelle. The 'high Elianes' were held by 1,150 (from II/1 RCP, 5 BPVN, and I/13 DBLE); the 'low Elianes' by 850 (III/3 RTA and BT 2); Épervier by 530 (8 BPC plus *c*. 140 from 5 BPVN and BT 2); Junon by 180 (miscellaneous); Liliane 1, 2, and 3 by 390 (I/4 RTM); Huguette 2, 3, and 5 by 600 (BMEP); and Claudine by 400 men (I/2 REI).

During the last week of April, Giap called his 381st AA Bn up from the lines of communication, and risked bringing some 37mm batteries closer to surround the reduced perimeter. A few new Chinese 75mm RCLs arrived, and were divided between his divisions (see above, *Orders of Battle/VPA*).

On 30 April an unheralded morning attack on Dominique 3 was driven off. There was much harder fighting at Huguette 5 on the night of 30 April/1 May; the strongpoint actually fell to part of 88th Regt, but was eventually retaken at 1000hrs on the 1st by *légionnaires* of the BMEP and I/2 REI.

Between 17 April and 1 May the garrison had suffered a net loss of 754 men. Most battalions had only 300–400 exhausted survivors, eating whatever chance finds they could gather from scattered air-drops, and kept on their feet by Benzedrine tablets. Apart from those holding perimeters, the 'reserves' to meet the next assaults numbered four weak companies. There were now only three mobile tanks in the main camp ('Mulhouse', 'Ettlingen', and 'Posen'), two with turret damage, and all subject to frequent breakdowns of their worn-out main guns.

THIRD ASSAULT PHASE: 1–6 MAY

Giap still did not underestimate the task of finally crushing GONO, and planned his May Day assault only to capture selected strongpoints before a four-day pause to consolidate. On the first night 308th Div was to eliminate the isolated Huguette 5; 312th Div was to take Dominique 3 (from which the artillery battery had long been withdrawn to Claudine), and to cut off

Eliane 1; and 316th Div was to capture Eliane 1, and mount a 'creeping siege' of Eliane 4. Meanwhile, 304th Div was to harass Isabelle and suppress its howitzer fire. Thereafter, the troops were to concentrate on preparations to meet French counter-attacks.

On the evening of 1 May, while part of 36th Regt made a diversionary attack on Liliane 3, 29th and 322nd Bns/88th Regt pounced on the weak BMEP company holding Huguette 5. A shell destroyed the CP, and the three internal trenches were soon penetrated; an attempted reinforcement was pinned down by fire, and the strongpoint fell at about 0200hrs.

On the eastern face, Eliane 1 was lost at about the same time (see commentary to battlescene on page 76 for details of this action). Eliane 2 was attacked by part of 174th Regt mainly to keep the defenders from I and III/13 DBLE from interfering with work on a mine tunnel that the VPA had been digging for some time. Several bunkers were taken, or destroyed by newly arrived 75mm RCLs, but unsuccessful attempts to reach the vital summit positions were limited to 'human bomb' volunteers.

At Dominique 3, the remaining southern positions were defended that night by a company each from 6 BPC and BT 2. They held off the first two assaults by 154th and 166th Bns/209th Regt, and resisted the third in hand-to-hand fighting before calling down mortar fire on their own positions. The strongpoint was overrun at about 0200hrs, after six hours of fighting. In all, the night cost GONO 489 casualties, thus destroying Langlais' meagre reserve, and left the remaining Eliane 4 and Eliane 2 dangerously outflanked.

Isabelle, 31 March–7/8 May 1954

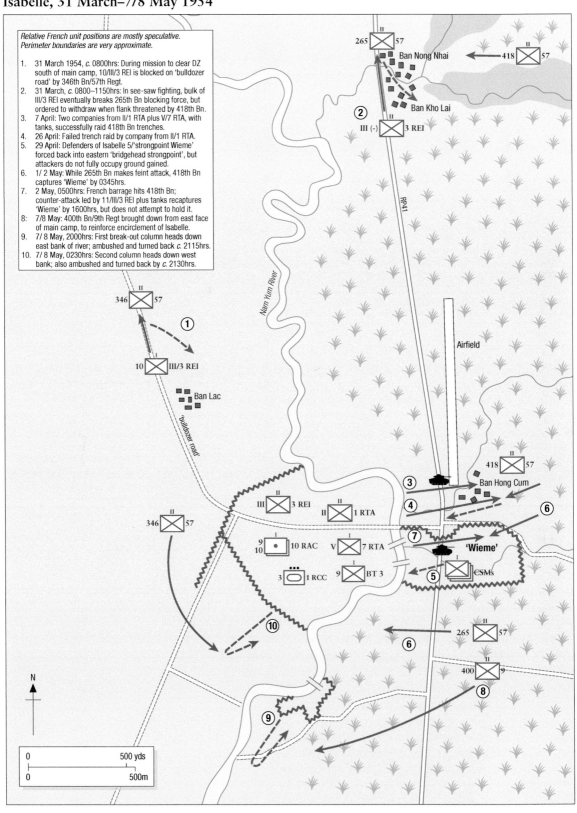

Relative French unit positions are mostly speculative. Perimeter boundaries are very approximate.

1. 31 March 1954, c. 0800hrs: During mission to clear DZ south of main camp, 10/III/3 REI is blocked on 'bulldozer road' by 346th Bn/57th Regt.
2. 31 March, c. 0800–1150hrs: In see-saw fighting, bulk of III/3 REI eventually breaks 265th Bn blocking force, but ordered to withdraw when flank threatened by 418th Bn.
3. 7 April: Two companies from II/1 RTA plus V/7 RTA, with tanks, successfully raid 418th Bn trenches.
4. 26 April: Failed trench raid by company from II/1 RTA.
5. 29 April: Defenders of Isabelle 5/'strongpoint Wieme' forced back into eastern 'bridgehead strongpoint', but attackers do not fully occupy ground gained.
6. 1/ 2 May: While 265th Bn makes feint attack, 418th Bn captures 'Wieme' by 0345hrs.
7. 2 May, 0500hrs: French barrage hits 418th Bn; counter-attack led by 11/III/3 REI plus tanks recaptures 'Wieme' by 1600hrs, but does not attempt to hold it.
8. 7/8 May: 400th Bn/9th Regt brought down from east face of main camp, to reinforce encirclement of Isabelle.
9. 7/ 8 May, 2000hrs: First break-out column heads down east bank of river; ambushed and turned back c. 2115hrs.
10. 7/ 8 May, 0230hrs: Second column heads down west bank; also ambushed and turned back by c. 2130hrs.

ISABELLE ALONE

From the second week of April, when 888th Bn/176th Regt was shifted up to face the Elianes, Isabelle's then 1,600-strong garrison probably outnumbered the remaining 57th Regt, which never fully encircled it. That regiment's 346th Bn entrenched west of the river, and 418th and 265th Bns to the north-east and south-east respectively. On 3 April, Lt.-Col. Lalande had the Algerian II/1 RTA (545 all ranks) plus 116 of the V/7 RTA survivors from Gabrielle; the Legion's III/3 REI (426); and about 410 Thais of 9/BT 3 and five CSMs. Sources are contradictory about the internal dispositions of the infantry, but at least initially the Legion battalion was in the west and the Algerians in the east of the main position. Most fighting actually took place beyond the 'bridgehead strongpoint' on the swampy east bank of the Nam Yum, for 'Isabelle 5' or 'Strongpoint Wieme' – named after the lieutenant commanding the Thai auxiliaries initially located there.

Isabelle's reason for existence was its two 105mm batteries from III/10 RAC. While the howitzers in Claudine and Dominique 4 could fire in support of Isabelle, its own batteries were best placed to create 'beaten zones' across the eastern approaches to the 'high Elianes'. (These batteries were actually overstrength, with 11 howitzers after the dropping of replacements and spare parts.) The Moroccan gunners continued to play a vital part in the artillery duel for the Elianes throughout April, despite coming under frequent bombardment themselves. Keeping them resupplied with shells, spare parts, and casualty replacements was difficult; occupying the DZ south of the small position required sorties in multi-company strength.

The CR also housed the three tanks of Lt. Préaud's Green Ptn, which had been prominent during the March battles to keep RP41 open. These emerged to make circuits of the perimeter most days; and during April Legion and Algerian companies with tank support often mounted aggressive sorties to wreck VPA trenches and 'aerate' Isabelle – initially with some success, but at higher cost in the second half of the month. Patrols clashed on most nights, as encroaching trenches increasingly threatened Isabelle 5.

'Auerstaedt', Lt. Préaud's M24 command tank of Green Ptn at CR Isabelle; note double radio antennae and spotlight, but camouflage obscures the turret name. The platoon took part in fierce road-opening actions north of Isabelle during late March, and against 57th Regt's trenches around the CR during April. 'Auerstaedt' and 'Ratisbonne' supported the internal counter-attack that retook Isabelle 5/Strongpoint Wieme on 2 May. (Photo General Henri Préaud, courtesy Simon Dunstan)

On 1/2 May a heavy artillery, mortar, and RCL bombardment disabled five of Isabelle's howitzers and smashed the rudimentary defences in Strongpoint Wieme. By 0345hrs assaults by 418th Bn had driven the scratch Algerian/Legion company that defended it that night back into the 'bridgehead strongpoint' on the east bank of the river. However, at 0500hrs a barrage from the main camp's artillery allowed Lt.-Col. Lalande to launch tank-led counter-attacks, which had recaptured the lost ground by 1600hrs. The physical condition of Wieme by now made it untenable, and only OPs were reinstalled.

Although shelled heavily, Isabelle was not assaulted thereafter. On the night of 7/8 May two mixed columns tried to break out southwards along the banks of the Nam Yum, but both failed. With 250 wounded to protect, at 0150hrs Lt.-Col. Lalande surrendered.

On 2 May Giap paused; his artillery stocks were modest, and he presumably expected the counter-attacks which Langlais no longer had the men to attempt. Bad weather severely limited French resupply drops, and although Maj.-Gen. Cogny had made the inexplicable and sacrificial decision to reinforce GONO at this desperate last moment with 1 BPC, only 107 paras managed to jump that night. From 3 May hundreds of walking wounded – including amputees – responded to an appeal to return to the front line, mostly in Junon and Eliane 11.

The night of 3/4 May brought another company or so of 1 BCP, but saw the final fall of Liliane 3. All three battalions of 36th Regt were committed from 0030hrs, but the defenders (1/I/4 RTM) managed to seal off the first attacks through infiltration tunnels. After desperate fighting, the last radio signal was cut off – by the death of the officer who was sending it – at 0335hrs, and an attempted counter-attack by 3/I/13 DBLE all the way from Eliane 3 failed. This brought 308th Div to within half a mile of the GONO

THIRD AND FINAL ASSAULT PHASES, 30 APRIL–7 MAY 1954

Giap had limited ambitions even for his May Day assaults, having learned to respect the impact of French counter-attacks by scrambled-together Legion and para companies. However, by 4 May his regiments had successfully eliminated the outlying Huguette 5 and Liliane 3 in the west, and Dominique 3 and Eliane 1 in the north and east. Lieutenant-Colonel Langlais no longer had the men to effectively reinforce strongpoints under assault, though he tried to send scratch companies all the way between the Huguettes and Elianes. In bitter fighting on the final night, 6/7 May, the VPA finally took Claudine 5 and the key bastion of Eliane 2. Remarkably, when morning broke on 7 May, some defenders were still holding out in Eliane 4, 10, and 12 – but GONO had no more to give.

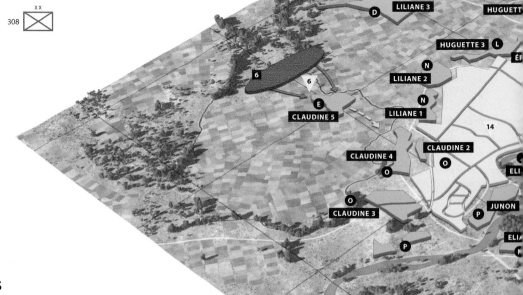

EVENTS

Note: key timings are provided in bold. Starting positions of VPA regiments are speculative.

30 April/1 May:

1. Huguette 5 penetrated by part of 88th Regt, but cleared by counter-attacking companies of BMEP and I/2 REI from Huguette 2 and Huguette 3, plus tanks. 4/BMEP takes over Huguette 5 from 8/BMEP.

1/2 May:

2. 1930hrs, remaining southern posts of Dominique 3 are attacked by 154th Bn/209th Regt from SE and 166th Bn/209th Regt from SW. Good support from artillery and Eliane 12 and Eliane 10, and reinforcements from 6 BPC and BT 2, prolong fighting on position; VPA forced to commit 130th Bn/209th Regt before strongpoint falls at **0200hrs**.

3. 2100hrs, 29th and 322nd Bns/88th Regt attack Huguette 5. Attempted counter-attack by 2/BMEP and part of I/2 REI fails to arrive before strongpoint falls at **0200hrs**.

4. From 2330hrs, Eliane 1 is attacked by 888th Bn/176th Regt from N, and by 439th Bn/98th Regt from W. Strongpoint falls at **0200hrs**, survivors falling back to Eliane 4.

3/4 May:

5. From 0030hrs, all battalions of 36th Regt assault Liliane 3. Penetrated at 0145–0200hrs, strongpoint falls at **0335hrs**, before attempted reinforcement by 3/I/13 DBLE all the way from Eliane 3 can arrive.

6/7 May:

6. From 2100hrs, 18th Bn (through tunnel) and 79th Bn/102nd Regt assault Claudine 5. Despite reinforcement by platoons of III/13 DBLE and I/2 REI from Claudine 4, strongpoint falls at **0130hrs**.

7. At Eliane 2, mine blown at 2030hrs; from 2100hrs, 249th Bn/174th Regt assaults up 'Champs-Elysées', and 251st Bn/174th Regt via new SW trench. Part of exhausted 255th Bn has to be committed before strongpoint falls at **0440hrs**. Reinforcement attempt by part of BMEP right across from Huguette 2 never arrives.

8. From 2030hrs, mixed para defenders of Eliane 4 are attacked from three directions by 215th and 439th Bns/98th Regt. Ground lost and recaptured in bitter fighting, and small BMEP reinforcement arrives from Huguette. Giap is obliged to authorize renewed 200-shell barrage, and commit battalion from fresh 9th Regt, before renewed assault at 0730hrs.

9. From 2030hrs, Eliane 10 holds off assaults by 115th Bn and part of 542nd Bn/165th Regt in savage see-saw fighting inside post. Reinforced c. 0300hrs by platoons of 8 BPC from Épervier, and later by Legion walking-wounded from Eliane 12, defenders still hold ground on morning of 7 May.

10. From 2100hrs, Eliane 12 holds off attacks by 130th Bn/209th Regt; defenders still hold ground on morning of 7 May.

7 May:

11. Final defenders of Eliane 4 are overrun at **c. 0930hrs**.

12. South-west tip of Eliane 10 finally falls at **c. 0930hrs**.

13. By **1500hrs** latest, defenders abandon Elianes 3, 11, and 12 and fall back across river. VPA shelling continues, but no further infantry fighting is confirmed by French sources.

14. GONO HQ orders ceasefire **c. 1630hrs.**

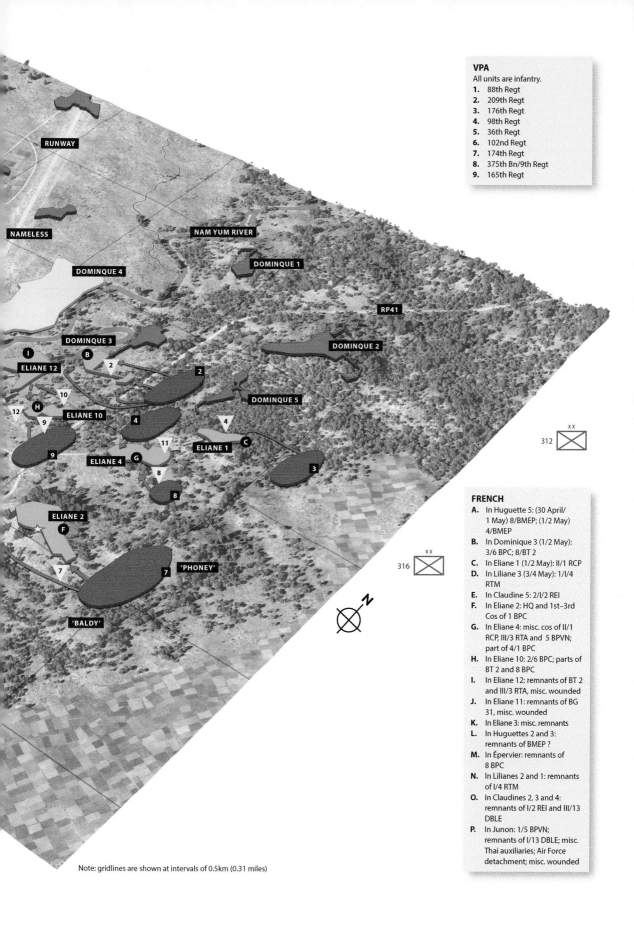

RUNWAY

NAMELESS

NAM YUM RIVER

DOMINQUE 4

DOMINQUE 1

RP41

DOMINQUE 3

DOMINQUE 2

I

B

ELIANE 12

2

2

10

DOMINQUE 5

12

H

ELIANE 10

4

4

9

4

11

C

ELIANE 1

9

ELIANE 4

G

3

8

ELIANE 2

8

F

7

7

'PHONEY'

'BALDY'

312 ⊠ xx

316 ⊠ xx

⊗ N

Note: gridlines are shown at intervals of 0.5km (0.31 miles)

VPA
All units are infantry.
1. 88th Regt
2. 209th Regt
3. 176th Regt
4. 98th Regt
5. 36th Regt
6. 102nd Regt
7. 174th Regt
8. 375th Bn/9th Regt
9. 165th Regt

FRENCH
A. In Huguette 5: (30 April/ 1 May) 8/BMEP; (1/2 May) 4/BMEP
B. In Dominique 3 (1/2 May): 3/6 BPC; 8/BT 2
C. In Eliane 1 (1/2 May): II/1 RCP
D. In Liliane 3 (3/4 May): 1/I/4 RTM
E. In Claudine 5: 2/I/2 REI
F. In Eliane 2: HQ and 1st–3rd Cos of 1 BPC
G. In Eliane 4: misc. cos of II/1 RCP, III/3 RTA and 5 BPVN; part of 4/1 BPC
H. In Eliane 10: 2/6 BPC; parts of BT 2 and 8 BPC
I. In Eliane 12: remnants of BT 2 and III/3 RTA, misc. wounded
J. In Eliane 11: remnants of BG 31, misc. wounded
K. In Eliane 3: misc. remnants
L. In Huguettes 2 and 3: remnants of BMEP ?
M. In Épervier: remnants of 8 BPC
N. In Lilianes 2 and 1: remnants of I/4 RTM
O. In Claudines 2, 3 and 4: remnants of I/2 REI and III/13 DBLE
P. In Junon: 1/5 BPVN; remnants of I/13 DBLE; misc. Thai auxiliaries; Air Force detachment; misc. wounded

HQ area, facing only the remains of I/2 REI in the waterlogged Claudines 5 and 4. The night cost the garrison another 222 casualties.

Only 74 men of 1 BPC jumped in on 4/5 May, and only 94 – the last to manage it – on 5/6 May. The fresh paras were entrusted with Eliane 2, where the sounds of digging from the mine had ceased. A good air resupply was achieved on the 6th, though at the cost of a mixed US–French C-119 crew shot down over Isabelle.

THE FINAL ASSAULTS: 6/7 MAY

Giap had received reinforcements, including 304th Div's 9th Regt brought up from his rear area, and Soviet multiple rocket-launchers. A ton of explosives had been packed into the Eliane 2 mine tunnel, whose detonation was supposed to signal that night's assaults: by 308th Div on Claudine 5, by 316th Div on Elianes 2 and 4, and by 312th Div on Elianes 10 and 12.

Daytime harassing shellfire and ranging 102mm rockets developed in the late afternoon into accurately focused bombardments of the target strongpoints, and destructive rocket salvos on the artillery positions. The mine at Eliane 2 went off at 2030hrs, but with only muted results; it was well short of the summit bunkers, causing relatively few casualties – and some confusion among VPA unit commanders. The ground assaults consequently began at 2100hrs, later than planned.

At Claudine 5, shelling by two mountain guns from short range was followed by attacks through tunnels and from nearby trenches by 18th and 79th Bns of 102nd Regt. The boggy strongpoint was defended by a company from I/2 REI, whose wire had been partly cut beforehand by Moroccan deserters. Despite reinforcement by platoons from III/13 DBLE and I/2 REI, the *légionnaires* were overrun by 0130hrs. The few survivors pulled back to block a communication trench to Claudine 4, with the help of miscellaneous engineers and gunners.

On Eliane 2, the new defenders from Capt. Pouget's 1 BPC would suffer from much-reduced supporting shoots, due to rapidly dwindling 105mm and 120mm ammo. The 174th Regt had now dug a trench from 'Baldy' to RP41, then northwards up the west of Eliane 2 to block reinforcements from Eliane 3. The 249th Bn advanced up each side of 'Champs-Elysées', and 251st Bn from the new western trench. Both took heavy casualties, but, under increasing pressure, Capt. Pouget had to call for reinforcements. Langlais ordered scratch companies from 8 BPC and the BMEP to attempt it, but, under mortar fire and infantry interception, none of them made it. Pouget's men were steadily pushed up to and beyond the summit, and by 0400hrs only 34 were left fighting. Two sergeants manned the .50-cal. MG on the hulk of 'Bazeille' shortly before Eliane 2 was finally overrun at 0440hrs on the 7th.

On the riverside flats, Eliane 10 was held by about 120 paras of 6 BPC plus a handful of Thais from BT 2. The attack by 115th Bn/165th Regt went in with little preparatory fire, and during prolonged and confused fighting inside the position they had to be reinforced from 542nd Bn. Reinforced by handfuls of paras from 8 BPC and of Legion walking wounded, the last defenders did not abandon the final south-west corner until 0930hrs on 7 May. Remarkably, the scratch garrison of nearby Eliane 12 successfully resisted botched attacks by 130th Bn/209th Regt.

The very last hilltop, Eliane 4, was – by the standards of that night – relatively strongly defended: by worn-down companies from II/1 RCP, III/3 RTA, 5 BPVN, plus one from 1 BPC, and the tanks 'Posen' and later 'Ettlingen'. It was attacked at 2030hrs by 215th and 439th

VPA troops examine the debris of battle shortly after the ceasefire, apparently in the southern edge of Épervier. Note the sabotaged and abandoned M24 tank 'Mulhouse', a US truck, and a wrecked F8F. This Chaffee had survived a hit by a 105mm shell, with a patch made from a mortar baseplate welded over the hole in the turret side. Most of the camp's squadron of Bearcats were destroyed by shellfire in the first 24 hours of the battle, only five managing to fly out safely on 13 and 14 March. (Collection Jean-Claude Labbe/Gamma-Rapho via Getty Images)

Bns/98th Regt, on three axes: from the north-west, across the saddle from Eliane 1, but mainly from the south-east. Although no artillery support was available, the 1 BPC and 5 BPVN troopers massacred their first attackers on the north and south faces respectively, and later penetrations were cleared by counter-attacks, aided by a reinforcement platoon that arrived from the BMEP. Giap was obliged to allocate another 200-shell artillery shoot, and 375th Bn from his fresh 9th Regt. The final assault lasted from 0730hrs until about 0930hrs, when Majs Bréchignac and Botella radioed their farewells. Under fire, the two tanks tried to escort the handful of survivors down to Eliane 10, only to find that it had already fallen.

Only handfuls of men from I/4 RTM, I/2 REI, III/13 DBLE, BMEP, 8 BPC, and other destroyed units now remained effective in the inner Huguettes, Lilianes and Claudines, Épervier, Junon, and Elianes 12, 11, and 3 – yet, even now, Giap did not immediately recognize that the west bank was indefensible. Most of his regiments had taken heavy casualties, and that morning good weather brought French ground-attack aircraft over the valley, so he paused again to take stock.

At about 1000hrs on 7 May, Brig.-Gen. de Castries agreed with Maj.-Gen. Cogny that he would attempt a previously discussed break-out by the strongest survivors that night. By perhaps 1500hrs, Elianes 12, 11, and 3 on the east bank had all been abandoned as indefensible. Before 1600hrs, de Castries was advised by his staff that GONO could not survive beyond nightfall, and that a break-out was suicidally impossible. From 1630hrs, unit commanders were ordered to destroy weapons, ammo, and equipment, and to cease fire.

At 1730hrs, the camp broadcast a radio message 'in clear' announcing a unilateral ceasefire. Major-General Cogny's last exchange with Brig.-Gen. de Castries bizarrely stressed that, for the sake of appearances, no white flags should be raised. Many were, as 308th and 312th Divs made an unresisted general advance across the camp from west and east. It was over at last.

* * *

While precise figures are impossible, plausible estimates of the garrison's casualties can be made. On 13 March GONO had a strength of 10,813, and

All the many propaganda photos published by the Viet Minh in the aftermath of the battle, purporting to be action shots of the final assaults, were actually staged on about 14–15 May. Here VPA infantry run northwards up the east bank of the river to the Bailey bridge, past some of the thousands of discarded parachute canopies that carpeted the battlefield after the random air-drops of the last few weeks. The French had left the single sculpted tree uncut, as a landmark for troops to find the bridge; just left of it, note Capt. Hervouët's abandoned M24 command tank 'Conti'. (Collection Jean-Claude Labbe/Gamma-Rapho via Getty Images)

4,277 men were parachuted in thereafter, giving a total of 15,090. Those known killed up to and including 5 May numbered 1,142; missing in action, 1,606; and wounded treated, 4,436 (of whom 429 had died) – giving a total of 7,184 casualties. In his authoritative study, Col. Rocolle estimates additional casualties during 6–7 May at 400 killed and 400 wounded. Total casualties before the surrender were thus just under 8,000, or very nearly 53 per cent of the reinforced garrison.

The VPA's losses have been widely disputed. The French estimated them at as high as 23,000, of whom 7,900 killed. Official Vietnamese figures at first gave 4,020 killed, 792 missing, and 9,118 wounded, for a total of 13,930; but figures released later suggest that the wounded may have totalled as many as 16,130 (though, due to vague wording, this figure perhaps includes men evacuated for sickness).

Details of the .50-cal. mount on the turret identify this Chaffee as one of Red Ptn's, probably 'Posen' or 'Smolensk', sabotaged and abandoned on the west bank of the river on 7 May. The 'surrendering crew' in this staged photo are probably North African prisoners, or from among the 'rats of the Nam Yum' – the hundreds of internal deserters and disarmed Thais who survived as best they could on the riverbanks during the latter part of the siege. Accounts by French veterans suggest that both their numbers and their feral nature have been exaggerated. (Collection Jean-Claude Labbe/Gamma-Rapho via Getty Images)

AFTERMATH

While most of the captured garrison were soon starting death-marches of between 300 and 450 miles to the POW camps, the VPA played cat and mouse over the fate of the most seriously wounded. Eventually, French aircraft were allowed to evacuate nearly 900 casualties and medics by 1 June.

News of the fall of Dien Bien Phu had a catastrophic effect on French national morale, and although the purely military situation in Indochina as a whole was not yet impossible, it was inconceivable that French voters would allow the war to continue. At the Geneva Conference on 7 May, Foreign Minister Georges Bidault at once proposed the negotiation of a general ceasefire. On 4 June Gen. Navarre was dismissed and replaced by the Army chief of staff, Gen. Paul Ely. The Laniel government fell on 12 June, to be replaced by an administration led by Pierre Mendès France, and the new premier publicly made himself a hostage to achieving a ceasefire by 20 July.

Between 24 June and 17 July, two Mobile Groups (GMs 100 and 42) were wiped out in the Central Highlands of Annam. However, during 28 June–4 July, Col. Paul Vanuxem carried out a skilful fighting evacuation of the southern part of the Delta (Operation *Auvergne*), for a concentration around Hanoi and Haiphong.

A general ceasefire came into effect on 27 July, bringing the French-Indochina War to a theoretical end (though abandoned French soldiers were still being hunted down by the VPA many months later). Under its terms, Vietnam would be partitioned at the 17th Parallel just north of Quang Tri, with a 'demilitarized

French prisoners assembled in the headquarters area. A total of 78 survivors of GONO (but including only 19 Europeans) successfully escaped and evaded. The total captured during and at the end of the battle is reported as 11,721, of whom fewer than 2,900 (25 per cent) were combat troops, but some 4,500 were wounded. The VPA allowed the repatriation of 858 of the most seriously wounded and 27 medical personnel by the end of May. Since the proportion of those captured alive among the 1,606 defenders who were listed as missing cannot be known, we may guess that about 9,000 began the march to the distant prison camps, of whom some 3,500 were wounded. Virtually all of the latter died on the march or in the camps, along with hundreds more of their comrades. (Keystone France/ Gamma-Rapho via Getty Images)

Viet Minh propaganda photo of the release of French prisoners – provided at the last moment with new clothing, and attentive nurses – on 31 August 1954. In fact, the treatment of GONO prisoners had been utterly callous; only about 3,900 were released to the French, many of them in a physical condition recalling survivors of World War II Japanese captivity. Additionally, perhaps as many as 1,000 *légionnaires* from Iron Curtain countries had been directly repatriated; so a rough estimate of the GONO prisoners who died on the march or in the camps is perhaps 4,100 – some 57 per cent of the total, in four to five months. (Bettmann Archive via Getty Images)

zone' separating the Communist DRV in the north from a new Republic of Vietnam in the south. The French would withdraw from the north and the Viet Minh (ostensibly) from the south, and until 18 May 1955 the populations would enjoy free movement to relocate in either direction. With US help, at least 750,000 civilians, particularly Christians, fled south from Tonkin.

Exchanges of POWs would begin on 18 August 1954. Thousands of CEFEO prisoners were unaccounted for, and the state of many who were released was shocking, but the French government was not going to risk raising any obstacles to the smooth progress of withdrawal. The CEFEO left Hanoi, and the VPA 308th Div entered it, on 9 October 1954. In the south a new Catholic premier, Ngo Dinh Diem, would soon be installed by the US State Department and the CIA, thus sowing the seeds for the next Vietnam War.

The last CEFEO troops to leave Indochina embarked during April 1956. (The first coordinated attacks on French targets in Algeria by the Front for National Liberation had already taken place long before, on 31 October 1954.)

Freshly fitted out with clean uniforms and full leather equipment, *bo doi* of 308th Div enter Hanoi as the French depart on 9 October 1954. (National Archives Washington/ Photo 12/ Universal Images Group via Getty Images)

THE BATTLEFIELD TODAY

Dien Bien Phu can be reached from Hanoi by a brief flight (twice daily) or a day-long bus journey. Visiting as part of an organized group tour is advisable, since English-speaking guides are hard to find; and visitors are recommended to take their own history books for reference, rather than relying on what is available locally.

The airport and the modern town now cover much of the battlefield, making orientation as difficult for returning veterans as it is for tourists, and muddy ricefields and snake-infested scrubland discourage freelance exploration. The Bailey bridge has been moved south to replace the old wooden bridge. The summits of Dominiques 1 and 2 (hills 'E1' and 'D1') are the highest points, but tall trees on the shoulders interfere with the overview of the valley. While more distant, Gabrielle ('Doc Lap Hill') offers a better general vantage point.

This photo taken high on Eliane 2 in May 2014, looking roughly eastwards, shows the 'Champs-Elysées' approach sloping down in the right background towards the foot of 'Baldy'. In front of the modern buildings, visitors inspect the mine crater below the summit. (Hoang Dinh Nam; AFP/Getty Images)

During a visit in January 1994, retired Gen. Marcel Bigeard is overcome by emotion as he greets former Sgt.-Chief Rolf Rodel of III/3 REI, a German veteran who was instrumental in the building of the French memorial at Dien Bien Phu in time for the 40th anniversary. (Eric Bouvet/Gamma-Rapho via Getty Images)

Cemeteries of VPA dead at Eliane 2 ('Hill A1'), Gabrielle, and Béatrice ('Him Lam Hill') total nearly 4,000 graves, but of these only a handful are individually named. There is no French cemetery.

The major sights for visitors to the central area include a new museum in the town, roughly on the site of the former Eliane 3; Brig.-Gen. de Castries' preserved HQ on its original site in Claudine; and, not far from it, a French memorial obelisk built in 1993–94. The museum displays many weapons and other artefacts, maps, dioramas, photos, and information boards with English translations, and a cinema shows a Vietnamese-language video. Unsurprisingly, the tone of all information is distinctly one-sided. One recent visitor describes it as more a good propaganda display than a true museum, and another notes some failures of 'curatorial rigour' – there is a certain amount of overlap between the French and US wars in Vietnam.

An 88-year-old veteran of the battle named Luu Ba Phat visits the victory memorial for the 55th anniversary in May 2009. (Hoang Dinh Nam; AFP/Getty Images)

The structure of Brig.-Gen. de Castries' HQ has been physically consolidated, under a more recently erected external roof, but it contains little of interest. The French memorial obelisk a few hundred yards away was negotiated and erected in the early 1990s by the efforts – and at the expense – of an individual Legion veteran (though he was subsequently compensated by the French Indochina Veterans Association).

A major feature of any tour is Eliane 2 ('Hill A1'), which has a visitor centre and improved access to the hilltop, as well as French unit-badge memorials. At the foot of the hill are a VPA cemetery and a Wall of Remembrance

Vietnam People's Army cemetery at Dien Bien Phu, photographed in 2014. (Hoang Dinh Nam; AFP/Getty Images)

bearing names, and a fenced collection of major equipment relics. While new buildings have been erected on the hill, above slopes which are now heavily overgrown, the view down 'Champs-Elysées' still gives a striking impression of the short ranges over which the fighting took place. The mine crater near the top of 'Champs-Elysées' is clearly evident; despite its relative failure, the digging of this mine is commemorated as a significant achievement. Warrant Officer Carette's M24 tank 'Bazeille' still sits on the summit, though now under an added roof which hampers photography.

Extensive trench lines and about a dozen bunkers have been reconstructed on Eliane 2 with concrete sandbags, but topography and vegetation make it difficult for the visitor to grasp many of the original military specifics of the position. In 2020 Alan Rooney reported that these are more evident from similar works on Béatrice, and that reconstructions have also taken place on Gabrielle and Anne-Maries 1 and 2.

Apart from 'Bazeille' on Eliane 2, when the 1 RCC veterans Gens. Préaud and Mengelle returned to the battlefield in 1995 they found three other 'bisons' displayed outside the old museum, and were able to identify four more scattered in individual locations. The following year Kieran Lynch also found wrecked 105mm howitzers and a 155mm in the old artillery area, and the remains of a quad-.50-cal. mount on the site of Junon, all supported on concrete bases. In the years since then a progressive process of 'tidying up' has included the assembly of some of these relics in the above-mentioned fenced compound at Eliane 2.

Finally, Gen. Giap's reconstructed HQ at Muong Phang can also be visited by taking a fairly time-consuming 20-mile bus ride.

FURTHER READING

For reasons of space, I have repeated here only a few of the works listed in the bibliography of my book *The Last Valley* (2004 – see below), to which interested readers are directed for a far wider range of sources. I believe that Rocolle's *Pourquoi Dien Bien Phu?* (1968) remains an essential source for understanding the progress of the battle; but the most important recent work is undoubtedly *Valley of the Shadow* by Boylan and Olivier (2018), which is warmly recommended. The authors draw upon material newly released from North Vietnamese sources since 2004, including significant supporting tables and appendices, and also include informative aerial photos of some individual strongpoints. Their work has enabled me to correct in this text many errors in *The Last Battle*, mainly of VPA unit identification.

Adam, Éric and Patrice Pivetta, *Les Paras Français en Indochine 1945–1954* (Histoire and Collections, 2009)

Bail, René, *L'Enfer de Dien Bien Phu* (Éditions Heimdal, 1997)

Bergot, Erwan, *Les 170 Jours de Dien Bien Phu* (Presses de la Cité, 1979)

Boylan, Kevin and Luc Olivier, *Valley of the Shadow: The Siege of Dien Bien Phu* (Osprey Publishing, 2018)

Brancion, Henri de, *Dien Bien Phu: Artilleurs dans la Fournaise* (Presses de la Cité, 1993)

Clayton, Anthony, *The Wars of French Decolonization* (Longman, 1994)

Dutrône, Christophe, 'La Bataille de Dien Bien Phu' (1) and (2), in *Militaria* Nos. 232 and 233, November and December 2004

Fall, Bernard, *Hell in a Very Small Place* (Vintage Books/Random House, 1968)

Gallardo, Pablo, 'Le Bataillon Bigeard de retour à Dien Bien Phu, 16 Mars 1954', in *Militaria* No. 407, August 2019

Gaujac, Paul (ed.), *Histoire des Parachutistes Français* (Éditions d'Albatros/Société de Production Littéraire, 1975)

Giap, Vo Nguyen, *Dien Bien Phu* (9th edn; Thế Giói Publishers, 2009)

Labrousse, Pierre, *Le Méthode Vietminh: Indochine 1945–54* (Charles-Lavauzelle, 1996)

Mengelle, André, *Dien-Bien-Phu: Des Chars et des Hommes* (Lavauzelle, 1996)

Renaud, Patrick-Charles, *Aviateurs en Indochine: Dien Bien Phu* (Grancher, 2003)

Rocolle, Pierre, *Pourquoi Dien Bien Phu?* (L'Histoire Flammarion, 1968)

Roy, Jules (trans. Robert Baldick), *The Battle of Dien Bien Phu* (Faber and Faber, 1965)

various, *Dien Bien Phu vu d'en Face: Paroles de bo doi* (Nouveau Monde, 2010)

Windrow, Martin, *The Last Valley: Dien Bien Phu and the French Defeat in Vietnam* (Weidenfeld and Nicolson, 2004)

ACRONYMS AND ABBREVIATIONS

French unit abbreviations

Arabic numerals refer to company of battalion. E.g. 2/I/4 RTM = 2nd Co of 1st Bn of *Régiment de Tirailleurs Marocains*.

Roman numerals refer to battalion of regiment. E.g. I/2 REI = 1st Bn of *2e Régiment Étranger d'Infanterie*.

List of acronyms and abbreviations

AA	anti-aircraft
AAMG	anti-aircraft machine gun (12.7mm/.50-cal.)
ACM	*Antenne Chirurgicale Mobile* – Mobile Surgical Team
ACP	*Antenne Chirurgicale Parachutiste* – Parachute Surgical Team
ANV	*Armée Nationale Vietnamienne* – Vietnamese National Army (French-led)
BEP	*Bataillon Étranger de Parachutistes* – Foreign (Legion) Parachute Battalion
BG	*Bataillon du Génie* – Engineer Battalion
BMEP	*Bataillon de Marche Étranger de Parachutistes* – Foreign Parachute Marching Battalion
Bn	battalion
BPC	*Bataillon de Parachutistes Coloniaux* – Colonial Parachute Battalion
8 BPC	*8e Battaillon Parachutiste de Choc* – 8th Shock Parachute Battalion
BPVN	*Bataillon de Parachutistes Vietnamien* – Vietnamese Parachute Battalion
BT	*Bataillon Thaï* – Thai Battalion (Tonkinese *montagnards*)
Bty	battery
CCB	*Compagnie de Commandement et des Services* – HQ and Services Company
CEFEO	*Corps Expéditionnaire Français d'Extrême-Orient* – French Far East Expeditionary Corps
CEPML	*Compagnie Étrangère Parachutiste de Mortiers Lourdes* – Foreign (Legion) Parachute Heavy Mortar Company
CIP	*Compagnie Indochinoise Parachutiste* – Indochinese company within a para battalion
CIPLE	*Compagnie Indochinoise Parachutiste de la Légion Étrangère* – Foreign Legion Indochinese Parachute Company
CMAG	Chinese Military Advisory Group
CMMLE	*Compagnie Mixte de Mortiers Lourdes Étrangère* – Foreign (Legion) Composite Heavy Mortar Company
Co	company
CO	commanding officer
CP	command post
CR	*Centre de Résistance* – defensive location with grouped strongpoints
CSLT	*Compagnie Supplétif Légère Thaï* – Thai Light Auxiliary Company
CSM	*Compagnie de Supplétifs Militaires* – (Thai) Military Auxiliary Company
13 DBLE	*13e Demi-Brigade de la Légion Étrangère* – 13th Foreign Legion Half-Brigade (unique historical title for this regiment)

DRV	Democratic Republic of Vietnam; Communist-governed entity existing in parallel with French colonial regime from September 1945
DZ	drop zone
FOO	forward observation officer (artillery)
FTNV	*Forces Terrestres Nord-Vietnam* – Land Forces North Vietnam
GAACEO	*Groupe d'Artillerie Antiaérienne Coloniale d'Extrême-Orient* – Colonial Far East AA Battalion
GAP	*Groupement Aéroporté* – Airborne Brigade
GATAC	*Groupement Aérien Tactique* – Tactical Air Group
GCMA	*Groupement de Commandos Mixte Aéroportés* (French-led guerrillas; the 'airborne' was largely theoretical)
GM	*Groupe Mobile* – Mobile Brigade
GMMTA	*Groupement des Moyens Militaires de Transport Aérien* – Military Air Transport Group
GONO	*Groupement Opérationnel du Nord-Ouest* – Operational Group North-West, i.e. Dien Bien Phu garrison
HMG	heavy machine gun (.50-cal./12.7mm)
LMG	light machine gun (rifle-calibre squad weapon)
MRL	multiple rocket-launcher
NCO	non-commissioned officer (sergeant and above)
OP	observation post
PIM	'interned military prisoner', i.e. Vietnamese forced labourer serving with CEFEO unit
PLA	(Chinese) People's Liberation Army
POW	prisoner of war
PSP	pierced steel plates – prefabricated runway surface
Ptn	Platoon
RAC	*Régiment d'Artillerie Coloniale* – Colonial Artillery Regiment
RALP	*Régiment d'Artillerie Légère Parachutiste* – Parachute Light Artillery Regiment
RCC	*Régiment de Chasseurs à Cheval* – Light Horse Regiment (armoured)
RCL	recoilless gun (resembling 'bazooka' but with ground mount)
RCP	*Régiment de Chasseurs Parachutistes* – Parachute Light Infantry Regiment
REI	*Régiment Étranger d'Infanterie* – Foreign (Legion) Infantry Regiment
RICM	*Régiment d'Infanterie Coloniale du Maroc* – Morocco Colonial Infantry Regiment (mechanized)
RTA	*Régiment de Tirailleurs Algériens* – Algerian Rifles Regiment
RTM	*Régiment de Tirailleurs Marocains* – Moroccan Rifles Regiment
Sept Regt	separate, i.e. non-divisional VPA regiment
SMG	sub-machine gun (pistol calibre)
VPA	Vietnamese People's Army (of Democratic Republic of Vietnam)

INDEX

Figures in **bold** refer to illustrations.